Expert ROS2 and Python for Autonomous Robotics

Advanced Techniques for Intelligent Systems, Machine Learning, and Multi-Robot Coordination

Thompson Carter

Rafael Sanders

Miguel Farmer

Copyright © 2025

Contents

Chapter 5: Python Programming for Robotics 122

How to Scan a Barcode to Get a Repository

1. **Install a QR/Barcode Scanner** – Ensure you have a barcode or QR code scanner app installed on your smartphone or use a built-in scanner in **GitHub, GitLab, or Bitbucket.**

2. **Open the Scanner** – Launch the scanner app and grant necessary camera permissions.

3. **Scan the Barcode** – Align the barcode within the scanning frame. The scanner will automatically detect and process it.

4. **Follow the Link** – The scanned result will display a **URL to the repository.** Tap the link to open it in your web browser or Git client.

5. **Clone the Repository** – Use **Git clone** with the provided URL to download the repository to your local machine.

Chapter 1: Introduction to Autonomous Robotics

Welcome to the World of Robotics

Overview of Autonomous Robotics

Have you ever wondered how self-driving cars navigate busy streets or how drones deliver packages with pinpoint accuracy? Welcome to the fascinating realm of **autonomous robotics**, where machines perform tasks without human intervention. But what exactly is autonomous robotics?

At its core, **autonomous robotics** involves creating robots capable of performing complex tasks independently. These robots leverage advanced algorithms, sensors, and artificial intelligence to perceive their environment, make decisions, and execute actions seamlessly. Whether it's a vacuum cleaner navigating your living room or a sophisticated industrial robot assembling products on a factory floor, autonomy empowers machines to operate efficiently and intelligently.

Imagine having a personal assistant that can anticipate your needs, manage your schedule, and even handle household chores—all without constant supervision. Autonomous robotics strives to bring this level of convenience and efficiency to various aspects of our lives.

Importance and Impact in Various Industries

Autonomous robotics isn't just a futuristic concept; it's revolutionizing multiple industries today. Let's explore how:

1. **Manufacturing and Industrial Automation**
   - **Streamlining Production:** Autonomous robots can work tirelessly on assembly lines, increasing production rates while maintaining high precision.
   - **Quality Control:** Equipped with sensors and vision systems, these robots can detect defects and ensure products meet quality standards.

2. **Healthcare**
   - **Surgical Assistance:** Robotic systems assist surgeons in performing intricate procedures with enhanced accuracy, reducing recovery times for patients.
   - **Rehabilitation:** Autonomous robots aid in patient rehabilitation, providing consistent therapy sessions and tracking progress.

3. **Logistics and Supply Chain**
   - **Warehouse Management:** Robots navigate warehouses, managing inventory, sorting packages, and optimizing storage solutions.

- o **Delivery Drones:** Autonomous drones deliver goods swiftly and efficiently, especially in areas where traditional delivery methods are challenging.

4. **Agriculture**

- o **Precision Farming:** Autonomous tractors and harvesters analyze soil conditions, plant health, and weather patterns to optimize crop yields.

- o **Pest Control:** Drones monitor fields for pests and apply treatments precisely, minimizing chemical usage and environmental impact.

5. **Transportation**

- o **Self-Driving Vehicles:** Autonomous cars and trucks promise safer roads, reduced traffic congestion, and lower transportation costs.

- o **Public Transit:** Autonomous buses and trains offer reliable and efficient public transportation options, enhancing urban mobility.

6. **Space Exploration**

- o **Robotic Explorers:** Autonomous robots traverse harsh environments on other planets, collecting data and conducting experiments where human presence is impractical.

- o **Satellite Maintenance:** Robots perform maintenance tasks on satellites, extending their operational lifespan and reducing the need for costly launches.

7. **Service Industry**

   o **Hospitality:** Autonomous robots can check guests in, deliver room service, and provide information, enhancing the guest experience.

   o **Retail:** Robots assist customers in finding products, managing inventory, and processing payments, streamlining retail operations.

Why ROS2 and Python?

Introduction to ROS2 (Robot Operating System 2)

Ever felt overwhelmed by the complexity of programming a robot to perform even simple tasks? Enter **ROS2**, your new best friend in the world of robotics. But what exactly is ROS2?

ROS2 (Robot Operating System 2) is an open-source framework that provides tools, libraries, and conventions to simplify the task of creating complex and robust robot behavior across a wide variety of robotic platforms. Think of it as the operating system for robots, much like Windows or macOS is for your computer.

Key Features of ROS2:

1. **Modularity:** ROS2 breaks down robot functionalities into small, manageable nodes that can be developed, tested, and maintained independently.

2. **Communication Infrastructure:** It offers a robust communication system that allows these nodes to communicate seamlessly, whether they're running on the same machine or distributed across multiple devices.

3. **Scalability:** Whether you're working on a single robot or a fleet of robots, ROS2 scales effortlessly to meet your needs.

4. **Community and Ecosystem:** With a vast community of developers and a rich ecosystem of packages, ROS2 provides solutions to a myriad of robotics challenges out-of-the-box.

Imagine trying to build a car from scratch without any of the essential components like the engine, transmission, or steering system. It would be daunting, right? Similarly, ROS2 provides the essential components and infrastructure, allowing you to focus on building innovative features rather than reinventing the wheel.

Advantages of Using Python in Robotics

Now, you might be wondering, **"Why Python?"** Great question! Python is a powerhouse in the programming world, and when combined with ROS2, it becomes an unstoppable force in robotics. Here's why Python is a preferred choice for many robotics projects:

1. **Simplicity and Readability:**

   o Python's syntax is clear and concise, making it easier to write and understand code. This simplicity accelerates the development process, allowing you to prototype quickly.

2. **Extensive Libraries and Frameworks:**

   o Python boasts a rich ecosystem of libraries, such as NumPy for numerical computations, OpenCV for computer vision, and TensorFlow for machine learning. These libraries can be seamlessly integrated into your robotics projects.

3. **Rapid Prototyping:**

   o Python's dynamic nature and extensive libraries enable rapid development and testing of new ideas, which is crucial in the fast-paced field of robotics.

4. **Community Support:**

   o With a massive global community, Python offers abundant resources, tutorials, and forums where you can seek help and share knowledge.

5. **Integration Capabilities:**

   o Python can easily interface with other programming languages and hardware components, providing flexibility in developing complex robotic systems.

6. ROS2 Compatibility:

○ ROS2 provides excellent support for Python, allowing you to write ROS2 nodes, manage packages, and utilize ROS2 tools effortlessly.

Diagram 1: ROS2 vs. ROS1 Architecture

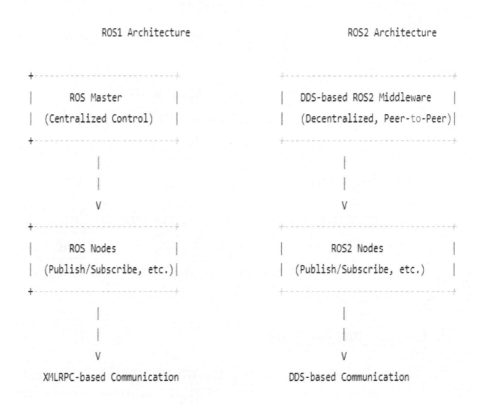

Description: This diagram contrasts ROS2 with its predecessor, ROS1, highlighting the architectural improvements and new features introduced in ROS2. Key differences include enhanced real-time capabilities, improved security, multi-robot support, and better performance on modern hardware.

How to Use This Book

Structure and Layout

Welcome aboard! This book is designed to be your comprehensive guide to mastering ROS2 and Python for autonomous robotics. Here's how it's structured to facilitate your learning journey:

1. **Progressive Learning Curve:**

   o **Beginners:** Start with the basics, ensuring you have a solid foundation.

   o **Intermediate Learners:** Dive deeper into more complex topics, building on your existing knowledge.

   o **Professionals and Hobbyists:** Explore advanced techniques and cutting-edge applications to enhance your expertise.

2. **Hands-On Projects:**

   o Each chapter includes practical projects that allow you to apply what you've learned. From building your first ROS2 node to developing sophisticated multi-robot coordination systems, these projects reinforce your skills through real-world application.

3. **Actionable Insights:**

   o Gain valuable tips, best practices, and troubleshooting strategies that you can directly apply to your work or personal projects.

4. **Visual Aids:**

   o Diagrams, illustrations, and code snippets are interspersed throughout the chapters to simplify complex concepts and provide clear guidance.

5. **No Repetition:**

   o Each chapter introduces new material and builds upon previous content without unnecessary repetition, ensuring a streamlined and efficient learning experience.

Tips for Maximizing Learning

To get the most out of this book, consider the following strategies:

1. **Stay Engaged:**

   o Approach each chapter with curiosity. Ask yourself questions like, "How can I apply this concept?" or "What real-world problems can this solve?"

2. **Hands-On Practice:**

- o Don't just read—code! Implement the examples and complete the projects to solidify your understanding.

3. **Take Notes:**

- o Jot down key concepts, commands, and insights. This will help reinforce your learning and serve as a handy reference.

4. **Experiment:**

- o Once you've completed the provided projects, try modifying them. Experimenting with different parameters and configurations can lead to a deeper comprehension.

5. **Join the Community:**

- o Engage with online forums, ROS2 communities, and Python groups. Sharing your progress and seeking feedback can accelerate your learning.

6. **Pace Yourself:**

- o Take your time to fully grasp each concept before moving on. Mastery comes with patience and persistence.

7. **Utilize Resources:**

- o Supplement your learning with additional resources such as online tutorials, documentation, and courses. The more perspectives you have, the better your understanding will be.

Final Thoughts

Embarking on the journey of autonomous robotics is both exciting and challenging. This book is designed to equip you with the knowledge and skills needed to excel in this dynamic field. By leveraging ROS2 and Python, you'll be empowered to create intelligent systems capable of transforming industries and enhancing our daily lives.

Remember, every expert was once a beginner. Embrace the learning process, stay curious, and don't hesitate to experiment. The world of autonomous robotics is vast and full of opportunities—your adventure starts here!

Summary

In this chapter, we've introduced the world of autonomous robotics, explored its significance across various industries, and discussed why ROS2 and Python are the perfect tools to master this field. With a clear structure, actionable tips, and engaging content, you're well on your way to becoming a robotics pro. Let's dive deeper in the next chapter, where we'll set up your development environment and lay the groundwork for your robotics projects.

Chapter 2: Setting Up Your Development Environment

Welcome to the next step in your autonomous robotics journey! Setting up a robust development environment is crucial for building, testing, and deploying your robotic applications effectively. In this chapter, we'll walk you through installing ROS2 on different operating systems, introduce Python tailored for robotics, and guide you in configuring your ROS2 workspace. Let's dive in!

Installing ROS2

Step-by-Step Installation Guide for Different Operating Systems

ROS2 (Robot Operating System 2) is the backbone of modern robotics development. It provides a flexible framework for writing robot software, offering tools and libraries to help you build complex and robust robotic applications. Installing ROS2 correctly is the first step toward creating intelligent autonomous systems.

But how do you get started? Whether you're using Ubuntu, Windows, or macOS, we've got you covered with detailed, easy-to-follow instructions.

Why Ubuntu?

Before we begin, it's essential to understand why Ubuntu is the recommended operating system for ROS2. Ubuntu offers robust support, extensive documentation, and compatibility with a wide range of ROS2 packages. While ROS2 can be installed on other operating systems, Ubuntu provides the most seamless experience.

Installing ROS2 on Ubuntu

Prerequisites:

- A computer running Ubuntu 22.04 (Jammy Jellyfish)
- Sudo privileges

Step 1: Set Up Your Sources List

First, ensure your system is up to date and install necessary packages:

```bash
```

```bash
sudo apt update && sudo apt install -y curl
gnupg2 lsb-release
```

Next, add the ROS2 GPG key to your system:

```bash
```

```
sudo curl -sSL
https://raw.githubusercontent.com/ros/rosdistro/m
aster/ros.asc | sudo apt-key add -
```

Add the ROS2 repository to your sources list:

```
bash
```

```
sudo sh -c 'echo "deb [arch=$(dpkg --print-
architecture)]
http://packages.ros.org/ros2/ubuntu $(lsb_release
-cs) main" > /etc/apt/sources.list.d/ros2-
latest.list'
```

Step 2: Update Your Package Index

Refresh your package index to include the new ROS2 repository:

```
bash
```

```
sudo apt update
```

Step 3: Install ROS2

You have multiple installation options depending on your needs:

1. **Desktop Install (Recommended):** This includes ROS2, RViz, demos, and tutorials.

```
bash
```

```
sudo apt install -y ros-foxy-desktop
```

2. **ROS2 Base:** A bare-bones install with just ROS2 essentials.

bash

```
sudo apt install -y ros-foxy-ros-base
```

3. **Additional Packages:** Depending on your project requirements, you might need extra packages.

bash

```
sudo apt install -y ros-foxy-navigation2 ros-foxy-turtlebot3
```

Step 4: Environment Setup

To ensure ROS2 commands are available in your terminal sessions, source the setup file:

bash

```
echo "source /opt/ros/foxy/setup.bash" >> ~/.bashrc
source ~/.bashrc
```

Step 5: Verify Installation

Confirm that ROS2 is installed correctly by running:

bash

```
ros2 run demo_nodes_cpp talker
```

If you see output indicating that a talker node is publishing messages, congratulations! ROS2 is successfully installed on your Ubuntu system.

Installing ROS2 on Windows

While Ubuntu is the preferred OS for ROS2, Windows users can also set up ROS2 with a few additional steps.

Prerequisites:

- Windows 10 (64-bit) or later

- Visual Studio 2019 or later

- Chocolatey package manager

Step 1: Install Chocolatey

Chocolatey simplifies the installation of software on Windows. Open PowerShell as an administrator and run:

```
powershell


Set-ExecutionPolicy Bypass -Scope Process -Force;
`
[System.Net.ServicePointManager]::SecurityProtoco
l = `
[System.Net.ServicePointManager]::SecurityProtoco
l -bor 3072; `
iex ((New-Object
System.Net.WebClient).DownloadString('https://com
munity.chocolatey.org/install.ps1'))
```

Step 2: Install Dependencies

Use Chocolatey to install necessary dependencies:

powershell

```
choco install -y git python3 wget cmake
```

Step 3: Download and Install ROS2

Visit the official ROS2 Windows installation guide for the most recent instructions. The general steps include downloading the ROS2 binary, extracting it, and setting environment variables.

Step 4: Environment Setup

Add ROS2 to your system PATH by editing environment variables. This allows you to use ROS2 commands from the Command Prompt or PowerShell.

Step 5: Verify Installation

Open a new Command Prompt and run:

powershell

```
ros2 run demo_nodes_py talker
```

If the talker node starts publishing messages, your Windows installation is successful.

Installing ROS2 on macOS

macOS support for ROS2 is more experimental compared to Ubuntu and Windows. However, you can still set it up with the following steps.

Prerequisites:

- macOS Catalina (10.15) or later

- Homebrew package manager

Step 1: Install Homebrew

If you haven't already, install Homebrew by running:

bash

```
/bin/bash -c "$(curl -fsSL
https://raw.githubusercontent.com/Homebrew/instal
l/HEAD/install.sh)"
```

Step 2: Install Dependencies

Use Homebrew to install necessary packages:

bash

```
brew install wget cmake python3
```

Step 3: Download ROS2 Source

Clone the ROS2 repository:

bash

```
mkdir -p ~/ros2_ws/src
```

```
cd ~/ros2_ws/src
git clone https://github.com/ros2/ros2.git -b
foxy
```

Step 4: Install ROS2 Dependencies

Use rosdep to install dependencies:

```
bash
```

```
sudo rosdep init
rosdep update
rosdep install --from-paths src --ignore-src -r -
y
```

Step 5: Build ROS2

Navigate to your workspace and build ROS2:

```
bash
```

```
cd ~/ros2_ws
colcon build
```

Step 6: Environment Setup

Source the ROS2 setup script:

```
bash
```

```
source install/setup.bash
```

Step 7: Verify Installation

Run a demo node to ensure everything is set up correctly:

```
bash
```

```
ros2 run demo_nodes_py talker
```

If the talker node publishes messages, your macOS installation is successful.

Python for Robotics

Python Basics Tailored for Robotics Applications

Python has become the go-to language for robotics due to its simplicity, versatility, and extensive library support. Whether you're a seasoned programmer or just starting, Python's readability and ease of use make it perfect for developing complex robotic applications.

But how does Python fit into the robotics landscape? Let's explore.

Why Python?

- **Ease of Learning:** Python's straightforward syntax allows developers to focus on solving problems rather than grappling with complex code structures.

- **Rapid Development:** Python enables quick prototyping and iteration, essential for the fast-paced world of robotics.

- **Extensive Libraries:** From machine learning to computer vision, Python's vast ecosystem provides tools to tackle virtually any robotics challenge.

- **Community Support:** A vibrant community means abundant resources, tutorials, and support are available to help you overcome obstacles.

Core Python Concepts for Robotics

To get you started, here's a crash course on essential Python concepts tailored for robotics:

1. **Variables and Data Types:**

    o **Numbers:** Integers and floating-point numbers.

    o **Strings:** Text data, useful for handling sensor data and logs.

    o **Lists and Tuples:** Ordered collections for managing multiple items.

    o **Dictionaries:** Key-value pairs for efficient data retrieval.

2. **Control Structures:**

    o **Conditional Statements:** if, elif, else for decision-making.

    o **Loops:** for and while loops for iterative tasks.

3. **Functions:**

    o Encapsulate reusable code blocks.

o   Enhance code readability and maintainability.

4. **Classes and Object-Oriented Programming (OOP):**

   o   **Classes:** Define blueprints for objects.

   o   **Inheritance:** Create hierarchies and promote code reuse.

   o   **Polymorphism:** Implement flexibility in code behavior.

5. **Exception Handling:**

   o   Manage errors gracefully using try, except, finally blocks.

6. **Modules and Packages:**

   o   Organize code into manageable units.

   o   Leverage Python's extensive library ecosystem.

Essential Libraries and Tools

Robotics development often involves integrating various functionalities like sensor data processing, machine learning, and real-time control. Python's libraries make these tasks manageable and efficient.

Key Libraries for Robotics:

1. **NumPy:**

   o   **Purpose:** Numerical computations and array manipulations.

- ○ **Use Case:** Handling sensor data, performing mathematical operations.

```python
import numpy as np

# Example: Creating a 3x3 matrix
matrix = np.array([[1, 2, 3], [4, 5, 6], [7, 8, 9]])
```

2. OpenCV:

- ○ **Purpose:** Computer vision and image processing.

- ○ **Use Case:** Object detection, image filtering, video capture.

```python
import cv2

# Example: Reading and displaying an image
image = cv2.imread('robot.jpg')
cv2.imshow('Robot Image', image)
cv2.waitKey(0)
cv2.destroyAllWindows()
```

3. TensorFlow/PyTorch:

- ○ **Purpose:** Machine learning and deep learning.

- o **Use Case:** Training models for object recognition, path planning.

```python

import tensorflow as tf

# Example: Building a simple neural network
model = tf.keras.Sequential([
    tf.keras.layers.Dense(128,
activation='relu'),
    tf.keras.layers.Dense(10,
activation='softmax')
])
```

4. **ROS2 Python Client Library (rclpy):**

- o **Purpose:** Interfacing with ROS2 using Python.

- o **Use Case:** Creating ROS2 nodes, publishing/subscribing to topics.

```python

import rclpy
from rclpy.node import Node

class Talker(Node):
    def __init__(self):
        super().__init__('talker')
        self.publisher_ =
self.create_publisher(String, 'chatter', 10)
```

```
        timer_period = 0.5
        self.timer =
self.create_timer(timer_period,
self.timer_callback)


    def timer_callback(self):
        msg = String()
        msg.data = 'Hello, ROS2!'
        self.publisher_.publish(msg)
        self.get_logger().info(f'Publishing:
{msg.data}')
```

5. **Matplotlib:**

   o **Purpose:** Data visualization.

   o **Use Case:** Plotting sensor data, visualizing robot paths.

```python
import matplotlib.pyplot as plt

# Example: Plotting sensor readings
sensor_data = [0.1, 0.4, 0.5, 0.7, 0.9]
plt.plot(sensor_data)
plt.title('Sensor Readings Over Time')
plt.xlabel('Time')
plt.ylabel('Reading')
plt.show()
```

6. **Pandas:**

- o **Purpose:** Data manipulation and analysis.

- o **Use Case:** Handling large datasets from sensors, preprocessing data for machine learning.

```python
python


import pandas as pd


# Example: Loading and displaying sensor data
data = pd.read_csv('sensor_data.csv')
print(data.head())
```

Development Tools:

1. **Integrated Development Environment (IDE):**

   - o **Recommended:** Visual Studio Code, PyCharm

   - o **Features:** Code completion, debugging tools, version control integration.

2. **Version Control:**

   - o **Git:** Essential for tracking changes, collaborating with others.

   - o **GitHub/GitLab:** Platforms for hosting repositories, managing projects.

```bash
bash


# Example: Cloning a repository
```

```
git clone
https://github.com/yourusername/robotics-
project.git
```

3. Virtual Environments:

- o **Purpose:** Manage project-specific dependencies without conflicts.

- o **Tools:** venv, virtualenv, conda

```bash
```

```bash
# Example: Creating and activating a virtual
environment
python3 -m venv my_robot_env
source my_robot_env/bin/activate
```

4. Docker:

- o **Purpose:** Containerize applications for consistent environments.

- o **Use Case:** Ensuring your robotics applications run the same way across different systems.

```bash
```

```bash
# Example: Running a ROS2 container
docker run -it osrf/ros:foxy-desktop
```

Diagram 1: Essential Python Libraries for Robotics

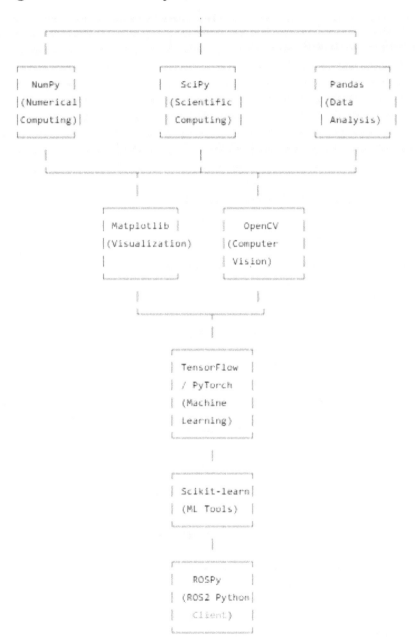

Description: This diagram showcases the key Python libraries integral to robotics development. It visually categorizes libraries based on their functionalities—numerical computations, computer vision, machine learning, ROS2 interfacing, data visualization, and data manipulation—highlighting how each contributes to building intelligent robotic systems.

Configuring Your Workspace

Setting Up ROS2 Workspaces

A well-organized workspace is the foundation of efficient ROS2 development. It allows you to manage your projects, dependencies, and build processes systematically.

What is a ROS2 Workspace?

A **ROS2 workspace** is a directory hierarchy where you build and manage ROS2 packages. It contains source code, build artifacts, and install files necessary for your robotic applications.

Creating Your First Workspace

Let's set up a basic ROS2 workspace step-by-step.

Step 1: Create the Workspace Directory

Choose a location for your workspace. Typically, it's placed in your home directory.

```bash

mkdir -p ~/ros2_ws/src
```

```
cd ~/ros2_ws
```

Step 2: Initialize the Workspace

Use colcon, the ROS2 build tool, to initialize and build your workspace.

bash

```
colcon build
```

Step 3: Source the Setup File

After building, source the setup file to overlay this workspace on your environment.

bash

```
source install/setup.bash
```

To make this permanent, add it to your .bashrc:

bash

```
echo "source ~/ros2_ws/install/setup.bash" >>
~/.bashrc
source ~/.bashrc
```

Step 4: Add Packages to Your Workspace

Navigate to the src directory and clone or create ROS2 packages.

bash

```
cd ~/ros2_ws/src
```

```
git clone
https://github.com/yourusername/your_ros2_package
.git
```

Step 5: Build the Workspace

Return to the root of your workspace and build.

```
bash
```

```
cd ~/ros2_ws
colcon build
```

Step 6: Verify the Workspace

Ensure that your packages are correctly built and sourced.

```
bash
```

```
ros2 pkg list
```

You should see your package listed among the ROS2 packages.

Managing Dependencies and Packages

Efficient dependency management ensures that your projects run smoothly without conflicts or missing components.

Understanding ROS2 Packages

A **ROS2 package** is the fundamental unit of software in ROS2. It contains nodes, libraries, data, and configuration files necessary for specific functionalities.

Adding Dependencies to Your Package

When developing a ROS2 package, you might need external libraries or other ROS2 packages. Here's how to manage them.

Step 1: Edit the Package Manifest

Navigate to your package's directory and open the package.xml file.

```bash
cd ~/ros2_ws/src/your_ros2_package
nano package.xml
```

Step 2: Add Dependencies

Within the <dependencies> tag, add the required packages.

```xml
<build_depend>rclpy</build_depend>
<exec_depend>rclpy</exec_depend>
<build_depend>std_msgs</build_depend>
<exec_depend>std_msgs</exec_depend>
```

Step 3: Update CMakeLists.txt (If Using C++)

For C++ packages, ensure that dependencies are found and linked.

```cmake
find_package(rclcpp REQUIRED)
find_package(std_msgs REQUIRED)
```

```
add_executable(talker src/talker.cpp)
ament_target_dependencies(talker rclcpp std_msgs)
```

Step 4: Install Missing Dependencies

Use rosdep to automatically install dependencies.

bash

```
cd ~/ros2_ws
rosdep install --from-paths src --ignore-src -r -
y
```

Step 5: Rebuild the Workspace

After adding dependencies, rebuild your workspace.

bash

```
colcon build
```

Diagram 2: ROS2 Workspace Structure

```
ros2_ws/
├── src/                    # Source code packages (your ROS2 packages)
│   ├── package_1/          # Package 1
│   │   ├── package.xml
│   │   ├── setup.py
│   │   ├── src/
│   │   └── ...
│   ├── package_2/          # Package 2
│   │   ├── package.xml
│   │   ├── setup.py
│   │   ├── src/
│   │   └── ...
│   └── ...                 # Additional packages
├── install/                # Installed files (generated after building)
├── build/                  # Build artifacts and intermediate files
└── log/                    # Log files from ROS2 nodes and builds
```

Description: This diagram illustrates the hierarchical structure of a ROS2 workspace. It highlights the src directory where all packages reside, the build directory generated by the build process, and the install directory containing built artifacts. The diagram also shows the relationship between these directories and how they interact during the build and run phases.

Summary

In this chapter, we've laid the groundwork for your autonomous robotics projects by guiding you through setting up your development environment. Here's a quick recap:

1. **Installing ROS2:**

   o Followed detailed steps for Ubuntu, Windows, and macOS.

   o Emphasized the importance of a correct installation to leverage ROS2's capabilities fully.

2. **Python for Robotics:**

   o Explored Python's role in robotics.

   o Introduced essential Python libraries like NumPy, OpenCV, TensorFlow, PyTorch, rclpy, Matplotlib, and Pandas.

   o Highlighted development tools such as IDEs, Git, virtual environments, and Docker.

3. **Configuring Your Workspace:**

   - Demonstrated how to create and manage a ROS2 workspace.

   - Explained dependency management and package organization for efficient development.

Next Steps

With your development environment set up, you're now ready to dive deeper into ROS2 fundamentals and start building your first robotic applications. In the next chapter, we'll explore the core concepts of ROS2, including nodes, topics, services, and actions, empowering you to create and manage complex robotic behaviors.

Final Encouragement

Setting up your development environment might seem daunting at first, but with the step-by-step guidance provided, you're well-equipped to tackle any challenges that come your way. Remember, every expert started where you are now. Embrace the learning process, stay curious, and don't hesitate to experiment. Your journey into the world of autonomous robotics has just begun—keep pushing forward!

Final Thoughts

Setting up your development environment is a foundational step in your autonomous robotics journey. By installing

ROS2, mastering Python for robotics, and configuring your workspace, you've established a solid platform to build, innovate, and excel in creating intelligent robotic systems.

As you move forward, remember that the development environment is your playground. Experiment, explore, and don't be afraid to tweak settings or try new tools. The more comfortable you become with your setup, the more efficient and creative you'll be in your projects.

Stay tuned for the next chapter, where we'll delve into the fundamentals of ROS2, exploring its architecture, communication mechanisms, and how to create your first ROS2 nodes. Get ready to bring your robotic ideas to life!

Chapter 3: ROS2 Fundamentals

Welcome to the heart of your autonomous robotics journey! In this chapter, we'll unravel the core components of **ROS2 (Robot Operating System 2)**, empowering you to build and manage sophisticated robotic systems. Whether you're a seasoned developer or just dipping your toes into robotics, this chapter is designed to provide clear, actionable insights into ROS2's architecture, communication mechanisms, and practical implementation using Python. Let's dive in!

Understanding ROS2 Architecture

Nodes, Topics, Services, and Actions

Imagine building a robotic system as orchestrating a symphony. Each musician (node) plays a specific instrument, contributing to the harmonious performance. In ROS2, **nodes** are the individual programs that perform tasks, **topics** are the communication channels through which nodes exchange information, **services** handle synchronous requests and responses, and **actions** manage long-running tasks that require feedback and the ability to cancel operations. Let's break these down further.

What is ROS2?

ROS2 is an open-source framework that provides a structured communication layer above the host operating systems of a heterogeneous compute cluster. It simplifies the task of creating complex and robust robot behavior across a variety of robotic platforms.

Key Components of ROS2 Architecture

1. **Nodes**

   o **Definition:** Nodes are the fundamental building blocks of a ROS2 system. Each node is an independent process that performs computation.

   o **Analogy:** Think of nodes as individual musicians in an orchestra, each responsible for playing a different instrument.

   o **Function:** Nodes can perform a variety of tasks, such as sensing, computation, and actuation.

2. **Topics**

   o **Definition:** Topics are named buses over which nodes exchange messages. They facilitate asynchronous, many-to-many communication.

   o **Analogy:** Topics are like radio frequencies where musicians (nodes) can broadcast and listen to music (messages) without direct interaction.

- o **Function:** Nodes publish messages to topics or subscribe to topics to receive messages.

3. Services

- o **Definition:** Services provide a synchronous, request-response communication model. They allow nodes to send a request and wait for a response.

- o **Analogy:** Services are like a conversation between two people where one asks a question and waits for an answer.

- o **Function:** Useful for operations that require confirmation or results, such as commanding a robot to move to a specific location.

4. Actions

- o **Definition:** Actions handle long-running tasks that provide feedback and can be preempted or canceled.

- o **Analogy:** Actions are akin to a performance that takes time, where the audience can see progress and even request changes during the show.

- o **Function:** Ideal for tasks like moving a robot arm to a position, where you might need continuous feedback or the ability to stop midway.

Diagram 1: ROS2 Communication Flow

```
+- - - - - - - - - - - - - - - - - - -+
|   Publisher Node          |
| (Publishes messages)   |
+- - - - - - - - - -+- - - - - - - - -+
                   |
                   |    (movement_commands topic)
                   v
+- - - - - - - - - -+- - - - - - - - -+
|   Subscriber Node         |
| (Receives messages to   |
|   control robot motion) |
+- - - - - - - - - - - - - - - - - - -+
```

Description: This diagram illustrates the flow of communication within a ROS2 system. It showcases how nodes interact through topics, services, and actions, highlighting the asynchronous and synchronous communication models.

Creating Your First ROS2 Node

Hands-On Tutorial: Hello World in ROS2 with Python

Ready to roll up your sleeves and create your first ROS2 node? Let's build a simple "Hello World" node using Python. This tutorial will guide you through the process step-by-step, ensuring you grasp the essentials of ROS2 node creation and execution.

Prerequisites

Before we begin, ensure you've completed the following:

1. **ROS2 Installation:** ROS2 should be installed on your system. Refer to Chapter 2 for detailed installation instructions.

2. **Python Setup:** Python 3.x should be installed, and rclpy (ROS2 Python client library) should be available.

3. **Workspace Configuration:** A ROS2 workspace should be set up and sourced. Refer to Chapter 2 for guidance.

Step 1: Create a ROS2 Package

A ROS2 package is a collection of nodes, libraries, and other resources. Let's create a package named hello_world.

1. **Navigate to the src Directory:**

bash

```
cd ~/ros2_ws/src
```

2. **Create the Package Using ros2 pkg create:**

```
bash
```

```
ros2 pkg create --build-type ament_python
hello_world
```

- ○ **Explanation:** This command creates a new ROS2 package named hello_world with ament_python as the build type, suitable for Python-based nodes.

Step 2: Structure of the Package

Your package directory should look like this:

```
arduino
```

```
hello_world/
├── hello_world/
│   ├── __init__.py
│   └── hello_node.py
├── package.xml
└── setup.py
```

Step 3: Writing the "Hello World" Node

1. **Navigate to the Package Directory:**

```
bash
```

```
cd ~/ros2_ws/src/hello_world/hello_world
```

2. Create hello_node.py:

Open hello_node.py in your preferred text editor and add the following code:

```python
import rclpy
from rclpy.node import Node

class HelloNode(Node):
    def __init__(self):
        super().__init__('hello_node')
        self.get_logger().info('Hello, ROS2!')

def main(args=None):
    rclpy.init(args=args)
    node = HelloNode()
    rclpy.spin(node)
    node.destroy_node()
    rclpy.shutdown()

if __name__ == '__main__':
    main()
```

- Explanation:
  - **Import Statements:** Import necessary ROS2 Python libraries.

- **HelloNode Class:** Inherits from Node and logs a "Hello, ROS2!" message upon initialization.

- **main Function:** Initializes ROS2, creates an instance of HelloNode, spins the node to keep it alive, and ensures clean shutdown.

3. **Make the Script Executable:**

bash

```
chmod +x hello_node.py
```

Step 4: Update setup.py

To ensure ROS2 recognizes your node, update the setup.py file.

1. **Open setup.py:**

bash

```
cd ~/ros2_ws/src/hello_world
nano setup.py
```

2. **Modify the setup Function:**

Replace the existing entry_points section with the following:

python

```
entry_points={
    'console_scripts': [
```

```
    'hello_node =
hello_world.hello_node:main',
    ],
},
```

- o **Explanation:** This defines a console script named hello_node that points to the main function in hello_node.py.

Step 5: Build the Package

1. **Navigate to the Workspace Root:**

bash

```
cd ~/ros2_ws
```

2. **Build the Workspace Using colcon:**

bash

```
colcon build --packages-select hello_world
```

- o **Explanation:** This command builds only the hello_world package, ensuring faster build times.

3. **Source the Setup File:**

bash

```
source install/setup.bash
```

- o **Explanation:** This makes the newly built package available in your current terminal session.

Step 6: Run the "Hello World" Node

Execute the node using the ros2 run command:

```
bash
```

```
ros2 run hello_world hello_node
```

Expected Output:

You should see the following message in your terminal:

```
css
```

```
[INFO] [hello_node]: Hello, ROS2!
```

Congratulations! You've successfully created and run your first ROS2 node using Python.

Communication in ROS2

Publisher and Subscriber Patterns

Effective communication is the lifeblood of any robotic system. In ROS2, nodes communicate primarily through **publishers** and **subscribers** using **topics**. Let's explore how these patterns work and how you can implement them in your robotic applications.

What are Publishers and Subscribers?

- Publishers:

- ○ **Definition:** Nodes that send out messages on a specific topic.

- ○ **Analogy:** Think of publishers as radio stations broadcasting music. They send out information without worrying about who is listening.

- ○ **Function:** Any node can publish messages to a topic, enabling information dissemination across the system.

- **Subscribers:**

  - ○ **Definition:** Nodes that receive messages from a specific topic.

  - ○ **Analogy:** Subscribers are like radio listeners tuning into a station. They receive and act upon the information being broadcasted.

  - ○ **Function:** Nodes subscribe to topics to receive relevant information and perform actions based on the received messages.

Implementing Publisher and Subscriber in Python

Let's create a simple example where one node publishes messages to a topic, and another node subscribes to that topic to receive and log the messages.

Step 1: Create the Publisher Node

1. **Navigate to Your Package Directory:**

```bash
bash

cd ~/ros2_ws/src/hello_world/hello_world
```

2. Create publisher_node.py:

```python
python

import rclpy
from rclpy.node import Node
from std_msgs.msg import String

class PublisherNode(Node):
    def __init__(self):
        super().__init__('publisher_node')
        self.publisher_ =
self.create_publisher(String, 'chatter', 10)
        timer_period = 1.0  # seconds
        self.timer =
self.create_timer(timer_period,
self.timer_callback)
        self.i = 0

    def timer_callback(self):
        msg = String()
        msg.data = f'Hello, ROS2! Count:
{self.i}'
        self.publisher_.publish(msg)
        self.get_logger().info(f'Publishing:
"{msg.data}"')
```

```
        self.i += 1


def main(args=None):
    rclpy.init(args=args)
    node = PublisherNode()
    rclpy.spin(node)
    node.destroy_node()
    rclpy.shutdown()


if __name__ == '__main__':
    main()
```

- Explanation:

  - **Publisher Creation:**
    self.create_publisher(String, 'chatter', 10)
    creates a publisher for the String message
    type on the chatter topic with a queue size
    of 10.

  - **Timer:** Sets up a timer to call
    timer_callback every second.

  - **Publishing Messages:** In timer_callback, a
    String message is created, published, and
    logged.

3. **Update setup.py:**

Add the new publisher node to console_scripts:

```python
python
```

```
entry_points={
    'console_scripts': [
        'hello_node =
hello_world.hello_node:main',
        'publisher_node =
hello_world.publisher_node:main',
    ],
},
```

4. **Make the Script Executable:**

```bash

chmod +x publisher_node.py
```

Step 2: Create the Subscriber Node

1. **Create subscriber_node.py:**

```python

import rclpy
from rclpy.node import Node
from std_msgs.msg import String

class SubscriberNode(Node):
    def __init__(self):
        super().__init__('subscriber_node')
        self.subscription =
self.create_subscription(
            String,
            'chatter',
```

```
            self.listener_callback,
            10)
        self.subscription  # prevent unused
variable warning


    def listener_callback(self, msg):
        self.get_logger().info(f'Received:
"{msg.data}"')


def main(args=None):
    rclpy.init(args=args)
    node = SubscriberNode()
    rclpy.spin(node)
    node.destroy_node()
    rclpy.shutdown()


if __name__ == '__main__':
    main()
```

- o Explanation:

    - Subscriber Creation:
      self.create_subscription(String, 'chatter',
      self.listener_callback, 10) creates a
      subscriber to the chatter topic.

    - Callback Function: listener_callback is
      invoked whenever a new message is
      received on the chatter topic, logging the
      received message.

2. **Update setup.py:**

Add the new subscriber node to console_scripts:

```python
```

```python
entry_points={
    'console_scripts': [
        'hello_node =
hello_world.hello_node:main',
        'publisher_node =
hello_world.publisher_node:main',
        'subscriber_node =
hello_world.subscriber_node:main',
    ],
},
```

3. **Make the Script Executable:**

```bash
```

```bash
chmod +x subscriber_node.py
```

Step 3: Build and Source the Workspace

1. **Navigate to the Workspace Root:**

```bash
```

```bash
cd ~/ros2_ws
```

2. **Build the Package:**

```bash
```

```
colcon build --packages-select hello_world
```

3. Source the Setup File:

```
bash
```

```
source install/setup.bash
```

Step 4: Run the Publisher and Subscriber Nodes

1. Open Two Terminal Windows:

- o **Terminal 1:** Publisher

- o **Terminal 2:** Subscriber

2. Run the Publisher Node:

In **Terminal 1**, execute:

```
bash
```

```
ros2 run hello_world publisher_node
```

Expected Output:

```
csharp
```

```
[INFO] [publisher_node]: Publishing: "Hello,
ROS2! Count: 0"
[INFO] [publisher_node]: Publishing: "Hello,
ROS2! Count: 1"
...
```

3. Run the Subscriber Node:

In **Terminal 2**, execute:

```bash
bash
```

```bash
ros2 run hello_world subscriber_node
```

Expected Output:

```csharp
csharp


[INFO] [subscriber_node]: Received: "Hello, ROS2!
Count: 0"
[INFO] [subscriber_node]: Received: "Hello, ROS2!
Count: 1"

...
```

Congratulations! You've successfully implemented the Publisher-Subscriber pattern in ROS2, enabling nodes to communicate seamlessly through topics.

Service and Client Interactions

While publishers and subscribers handle asynchronous communication, **services** and **clients** facilitate synchronous interactions where a request is sent, and a response is awaited. This is akin to asking a question and waiting for an answer.

What are Services and Clients?

- **Services:**

    - **Definition:** Nodes that offer specific functionalities upon request.

- Analogy: A service node is like a waiter taking your order in a restaurant.

- Function: They perform operations and return results based on client requests.

- Clients:

    - Definition: Nodes that send requests to services and wait for responses.

    - Analogy: A client node is like a diner placing an order with the waiter.

    - Function: They request specific services and handle the responses.

Implementing Service and Client in Python

Let's create a simple service that adds two integers and a client that requests this service.

Step 1: Create the Service Node

1. **Navigate to Your Package Directory:**

bash

```
cd ~/ros2_ws/src/hello_world/hello_world
```

2. **Create add_two_ints_service.py:**

python

```
import rclpy
from rclpy.node import Node
```

```
from example_interfaces.srv import AddTwoInts

class AddTwoIntsService(Node):
    def __init__(self):
        super().__init__('add_two_ints_service')
        self.srv =
self.create_service(AddTwoInts, 'add_two_ints',
self.add_two_ints_callback)
        self.get_logger().info('Service
"add_two_ints" is ready.')

    def add_two_ints_callback(self, request,
response):
        response.sum = request.a + request.b
        self.get_logger().info(f'Received
request: a={request.a}, b={request.b} |
Responding with: {response.sum}')
        return response

def main(args=None):
    rclpy.init(args=args)
    node = AddTwoIntsService()
    rclpy.spin(node)
    rclpy.shutdown()

if __name__ == '__main__':
    main()
```

- o **Explanation:**

- **Service Creation:**
  self.create_service(AddTwoInts,
  'add_two_ints', self.add_two_ints_callback)
  creates a service named add_two_ints
  using the AddTwoInts service type.

- **Callback Function:** add_two_ints_callback
  handles incoming requests by adding the
  two integers and setting the response.

3. **Update setup.py:**

Add the service node to console_scripts:

python

```
entry_points={
    'console_scripts': [
        'hello_node =
hello_world.hello_node:main',
        'publisher_node =
hello_world.publisher_node:main',
        'subscriber_node =
hello_world.subscriber_node:main',
        'add_two_ints_service =
hello_world.add_two_ints_service:main',
    ],
},
```

4. **Make the Script Executable:**

bash

```
chmod +x add_two_ints_service.py
```

Step 2: Create the Client Node

1. **Create add_two_ints_client.py:**

```python
import sys
import rclpy
from rclpy.node import Node
from example_interfaces.srv import AddTwoInts

class AddTwoIntsClient(Node):
    def __init__(self):
        super().__init__('add_two_ints_client')
        self.cli = self.create_client(AddTwoInts,
'add_two_ints')
        while not
self.cli.wait_for_service(timeout_sec=1.0):
            self.get_logger().info('Service not
available, waiting...')
        self.req = AddTwoInts.Request()

    def send_request(self, a, b):
        self.req.a = a
        self.req.b = b
        self.future =
self.cli.call_async(self.req)
```

```python
def main(args=None):
    rclpy.init(args=args)
    client = AddTwoIntsClient()
    client.send_request(int(sys.argv[1]),
int(sys.argv[2]))
    while rclpy.ok():
        rclpy.spin_once(client)
        if client.future.done():
            try:
                response = client.future.result()
            except Exception as e:

client.get_logger().info(f'Service call failed:
{e}')
            else:
                client.get_logger().info(f'Result
of add_two_ints: {response.sum}')
            break
    client.destroy_node()
    rclpy.shutdown()


if __name__ == '__main__':
    if len(sys.argv) != 3:
        print('Usage: ros2 run hello_world
add_two_ints_client.py a b')
    else:
        main()
```

- ○ **Explanation:**
  - ▪ **Client Creation:** self.create_client(AddTwoInts, 'add_two_ints') creates a client for the add_two_ints service.
  - ▪ **Sending Requests:** send_request assigns values to a and b and sends an asynchronous request.
  - ▪ **Handling Responses:** The client waits for the service to respond and logs the result.

2. **Update setup.py:**

Add the client node to console_scripts:

python

```python
entry_points={
    'console_scripts': [
        'hello_node =
hello_world.hello_node:main',
        'publisher_node =
hello_world.publisher_node:main',
        'subscriber_node =
hello_world.subscriber_node:main',
        'add_two_ints_service =
hello_world.add_two_ints_service:main',
        'add_two_ints_client =
hello_world.add_two_ints_client:main',
```

```
  ],
},
```

3. Make the Script Executable:

bash

```
chmod +x add_two_ints_client.py
```

Step 3: Build and Source the Workspace

1. Navigate to the Workspace Root:

```bash

cd ~/ros2_ws
```

2. Build the Package:

```bash

colcon build --packages-select hello_world
```

3. Source the Setup File:

```bash

source install/setup.bash
```

Step 4: Run the Service and Client Nodes

1. Open Two Terminal Windows:

- o **Terminal 1:** Service
- o **Terminal 2:** Client

2. Run the Service Node:

In **Terminal 1**, execute:

bash

ros2 run hello_world add_two_ints_service

Expected Output:

```
less
```

```
[INFO] [add_two_ints_service]: Service
"add_two_ints" is ready.
[INFO] [add_two_ints_service]: Received request:
a=2, b=3 | Responding with: 5
```

3. **Run the Client Node:**

In **Terminal 2**, execute:

```
bash
```

```
ros2 run hello_world add_two_ints_client 2 3
```

Expected Output:

```
css
```

```
[INFO] [add_two_ints_client]: Result of
add_two_ints: 5
```

Great job! You've successfully implemented the Service-Client pattern in ROS2, enabling synchronous communication between nodes.

Diagram 2: Publisher-Subscriber Model

Description: This diagram visualizes the Publisher-Subscriber communication model in ROS2. It illustrates how multiple publishers and subscribers interact through topics, showcasing the flow of messages from publishers to subscribers.

Summary

In **Chapter 3: ROS2 Fundamentals,** we've delved into the essential components that make ROS2 a powerful framework for autonomous robotics. Here's a quick recap of what we've covered:

1. **Understanding ROS2 Architecture:**

   o Explored nodes, topics, services, and actions.

   o Illustrated how these components interact within a ROS2 system.

2. **Creating Your First ROS2 Node:**

- o Built a simple "Hello World" node using Python.

- o Implemented Publisher and Subscriber nodes to facilitate communication.

3. **Communication in ROS2:**

   - o Implemented synchronous Service-Client interactions.

   - o Established the Publisher-Subscriber communication model.

4. **Visual Diagrams:**

   - o Provided conceptual diagrams to visualize ROS2 communication flow, node structures, and communication patterns.

Next Steps

With a solid understanding of ROS2's architecture and communication mechanisms, you're now ready to explore more advanced topics. In the next chapter, we'll delve deeper into **Advanced ROS2 Concepts**, including lifecycle management, parameter handling, and effective debugging techniques. These skills will enable you to build more resilient and efficient robotic systems.

Final Encouragement

Mastering ROS2 fundamentals is a significant milestone in your robotics journey. Remember, every complex system starts with understanding its core components. By grasping how nodes communicate and interact, you've laid the groundwork for developing sophisticated autonomous systems. Keep experimenting, stay curious, and don't hesitate to revisit concepts as you continue to build and refine your robotic projects. Your expertise in ROS2 is growing—keep pushing the boundaries!

Final Thoughts

Mastering ROS2 fundamentals is akin to learning the ABCs of robotics. With a solid grasp of nodes, topics, services, and actions, you're well-equipped to build and manage complex robotic systems. As you continue your journey, remember that hands-on practice is key. Experiment with different communication patterns, create diverse nodes, and explore ROS2's vast ecosystem to fully harness its potential.

Stay tuned for the next chapter, where we'll delve into **Advanced ROS2 Concepts**, enhancing your ability to manage node lifecycles, handle parameters dynamically, and debug your robotic applications effectively. Keep building, stay curious, and embrace the exciting challenges that come your way. Your path to becoming a ROS2 pro is well underway!

Chapter 4: Advanced ROS2 Concepts

Welcome to the next level of your autonomous robotics journey! In this chapter, we'll delve into the more intricate aspects of **ROS2 (Robot Operating System 2)**, equipping you with the knowledge and tools to build resilient, flexible, and efficient robotic systems. We'll explore **Lifecycle Management, Parameter Management**, and **Logging and Debugging**—three pillars that ensure your robots operate smoothly and adaptively in dynamic environments. Whether you're looking to optimize your robot's performance or troubleshoot complex issues, this chapter has you covered. Let's get started!

Lifecycle Management

Node Lifecycle and State Transitions

Have you ever wondered how complex systems manage their operations seamlessly, ensuring that each component behaves predictably? In robotics, managing the lifecycle of nodes is crucial for creating robust and reliable applications. **Lifecycle Management** in ROS2 provides a structured approach to controlling the states and transitions of nodes, ensuring that they operate correctly throughout their lifecycle.

What is Lifecycle Management?

Lifecycle Management refers to the systematic control of a node's state from its inception to termination. By defining specific states and transitions, you can manage how nodes initialize, become active, handle errors, and shut down gracefully. This ensures that your robotic system remains stable and predictable, even in the face of unexpected events or failures.

Key Concepts in Lifecycle Management

1. **Managed Nodes:**

   o **Definition:** Nodes that follow a predefined lifecycle with specific states and transitions.

   o **Analogy:** Think of managed nodes as well-trained employees who know their roles and responsibilities, transitioning smoothly between tasks without confusion.

   o **Function:** They ensure that resources are allocated efficiently and that the node behaves consistently across different operational phases.

2. **States:**

   o **Inactive:** The node is created but not performing any operations. It's a safe state to make configuration changes.

   o **Activating:** The node is transitioning from inactive to active. Resources are being allocated.

- o **Active:** The node is fully operational, performing its designated tasks.

- o **Deactivating:** The node is transitioning from active to inactive. Resources are being released.

- o **Finalized:** The node has been shut down and can no longer be reactivated.

3. **Transitions:**

- o **Configure:** Moves the node from inactive to activating, preparing it for operation.

- o **Activate:** Transitions the node from activating to active, enabling it to perform tasks.

- o **Deactivate:** Moves the node from active to deactivating, stopping its operations.

- o **Cleanup:** Transitions the node from deactivating to inactive, freeing resources.

- o **Shutdown:** Moves the node to the finalized state, terminating its lifecycle.

Benefits of Lifecycle Management

- **Predictability:** Ensures nodes behave consistently, reducing unexpected behaviors.

- **Resource Management:** Efficiently allocates and deallocates resources, optimizing system performance.

- **Error Handling:** Provides mechanisms to handle errors gracefully, maintaining system stability.

- **Scalability:** Facilitates the management of multiple nodes, essential for complex robotic systems.

Diagram 1: ROS2 Node Lifecycle States

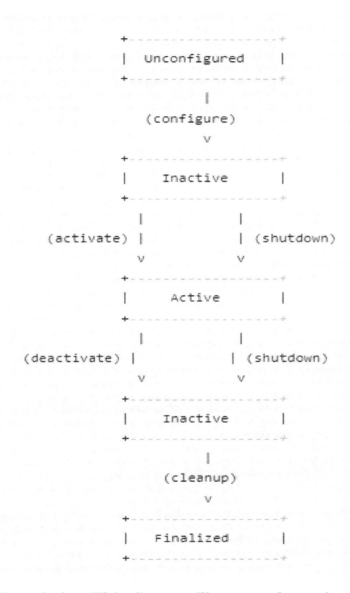

Description: This diagram illustrates the various states of a ROS2 node's lifecycle and the transitions between them. It highlights how a node moves from creation to active operation, handles deactivation, and eventually shuts down. Each state is connected by arrows indicating possible transitions, providing a clear overview of the node's lifecycle.

Implementing Lifecycle Management in ROS2

Now that we've understood the basics, let's see how to implement lifecycle management in ROS2 using Python.

Step 1: Creating a Managed Node

1. **Navigate to Your Package Directory:**

bash

```
cd ~/ros2_ws/src/hello_world/hello_world
```

2. **Create lifecycle_node.py:**

python

```
import rclpy
from rclpy.node import Node
from rclpy.lifecycle import LifecycleNode
from rclpy.lifecycle import State
from rclpy.lifecycle import TransitionCallbackReturn

class LifecycleExampleNode(LifecycleNode):
    def __init__(self):
```

```
super().__init__('lifecycle_example_node')

self.get_logger().info('LifecycleExampleNode has
been created.')

    def on_configure(self, state: State) ->
TransitionCallbackReturn:
        self.get_logger().info('Configuring...')
        # Initialize resources here
        return TransitionCallbackReturn.SUCCESS

    def on_activate(self, state: State) ->
TransitionCallbackReturn:
        self.get_logger().info('Activating...')
        # Activate publishers/subscribers here
        return TransitionCallbackReturn.SUCCESS

    def on_deactivate(self, state: State) ->
TransitionCallbackReturn:
        self.get_logger().info('Deactivating...')
        # Deactivate publishers/subscribers here
        return TransitionCallbackReturn.SUCCESS

    def on_cleanup(self, state: State) ->
TransitionCallbackReturn:
        self.get_logger().info('Cleaning up...')
        # Release resources here
```

```python
        return TransitionCallbackReturn.SUCCESS


    def on_shutdown(self, state: State) ->
TransitionCallbackReturn:
        self.get_logger().info('Shutting
down...')
        # Final cleanup before shutdown
        return TransitionCallbackReturn.SUCCESS


def main(args=None):
    rclpy.init(args=args)
    lifecycle_node = LifecycleExampleNode()
    executor =
rclpy.executors.SingleThreadedExecutor()
    executor.add_node(lifecycle_node)


lifecycle_node.trigger_transition(lifecycle_node.
configure())


lifecycle_node.trigger_transition(lifecycle_node.
activate())
    try:
        executor.spin()
    except KeyboardInterrupt:
        pass


lifecycle_node.trigger_transition(lifecycle_node.
deactivate())
```

```
lifecycle_node.trigger_transition(lifecycle_node.
cleanup())

lifecycle_node.trigger_transition(lifecycle_node.
shutdown())
    executor.shutdown()
    lifecycle_node.destroy_node()
    rclpy.shutdown()


if __name__ == '__main__':
    main()
```

- o **Explanation:**

  - **LifecycleNode Class:** Inherits from LifecycleNode, enabling lifecycle management.

  - **Lifecycle Callbacks:** Defines methods like on_configure, on_activate, on_deactivate, on_cleanup, and on_shutdown to handle state transitions.

  - **Main Function:** Initializes the node, triggers transitions, and manages the node's lifecycle.

3. **Update setup.py:**

Add the lifecycle node to console_scripts:

```python
python
```

```
entry_points={
    'console_scripts': [
        'hello_node =
hello_world.hello_node:main',
        'publisher_node =
hello_world.publisher_node:main',
        'subscriber_node =
hello_world.subscriber_node:main',
        'add_two_ints_service =
hello_world.add_two_ints_service:main',
        'add_two_ints_client =
hello_world.add_two_ints_client:main',
        'lifecycle_node =
hello_world.lifecycle_node:main',
    ],
},
```

4. **Make the Script Executable:**

```bash
bash
```

```
chmod +x lifecycle_node.py
```

Step 2: Building and Running the Lifecycle Node

1. **Navigate to the Workspace Root:**

```bash
bash
```

```
cd ~/ros2_ws
```

2. **Build the Package:**

bash

colcon build --packages-select hello_world

3. Source the Setup File:

bash

source install/setup.bash

4. Run the Lifecycle Node:

bash

ros2 run hello_world lifecycle_node

Expected Output:

less

```
[INFO] [lifecycle_example_node]:
LifecycleExampleNode has been created.
[INFO] [lifecycle_example_node]: Configuring...
[INFO] [lifecycle_example_node]: Activating...
```

- o The node transitions through the configure and activate states, logging each transition.

Step 3: Interacting with the Lifecycle Node

You can manually control the lifecycle transitions using ROS2's lifecycle commands.

1. Open a New Terminal and Source the Setup File:

bash

```
source ~/ros2_ws/install/setup.bash
```

2. List Available Lifecycle Nodes:

```bash

ros2 lifecycle nodes
```

Expected Output:

```bash

/lifecycle_example_node
```

3. Get the Current State of the Node:

```bash

ros2 lifecycle get /lifecycle_example_node
```

Expected Output:

```bash

/lifecycle_example_node is in state ACTIVE
```

4. Trigger a State Transition:

- **Deactivate the Node:**

```bash

ros2 lifecycle set /lifecycle_example_node
deactivate
```

Expected Output:

```bash

```

Successfully changed state of
/lifecycle_example_node to DEACTIVATING

- ○ **Check the New State:**

bash

```
ros2 lifecycle get /lifecycle_example_node
```

Expected Output:

bash

/lifecycle_example_node is in state INACTIVE

- ○ **Shutdown the Node:**

bash

```
ros2 lifecycle set /lifecycle_example_node
shutdown
```

Expected Output:

bash

Successfully changed state of
/lifecycle_example_node to FINALIZED

Best Practices for Lifecycle Management

- **Define Clear States:** Ensure that each state has a well-defined purpose and behavior.

- **Handle Transitions Gracefully:** Implement proper resource allocation and deallocation during state transitions to prevent leaks and ensure stability.

- **Monitor State Changes:** Use logging to track state transitions, aiding in debugging and system monitoring.

- **Automate Transitions:** Where possible, automate state transitions to reduce manual intervention and potential errors.

Parameter Management

Dynamic and Static Parameters

Ever needed to adjust your robot's behavior on the fly without stopping its operations? **Parameter Management** in ROS2 allows you to configure and modify node parameters dynamically or statically, providing flexibility and adaptability in your robotic applications. Let's explore how to manage parameters effectively in ROS2.

What are Parameters?

Parameters are configurable values that influence a node's behavior. They allow you to adjust aspects like speed, sensor sensitivity, or operational thresholds without altering the codebase. Parameters can be set at launch time or modified during runtime, offering both static and dynamic configuration options.

Dynamic vs. Static Parameters

1. **Static Parameters:**

- o **Definition:** Parameters set at the initialization of a node and remain unchanged during its lifecycle.

- o **Use Case:** Setting fixed values that don't require adjustment once the node is running, such as a robot's maximum speed.

- o **Example:** Configuring a constant speed for a delivery robot.

2. **Dynamic Parameters:**

- o **Definition:** Parameters that can be modified while the node is running.

- o **Use Case:** Adjusting operational settings in response to environmental changes or user input, such as altering sensor sensitivity.

- o **Example:** Changing the sensitivity of obstacle detection based on different lighting conditions.

Benefits of Effective Parameter Management

- **Flexibility:** Easily adapt to changing requirements without code modifications.

- **Reusability:** Create generalized nodes that can be customized for different applications through parameters.

- **Maintainability:** Simplify the process of updating node behaviors, reducing the risk of introducing bugs.

- **Efficiency:** Optimize robot performance by fine-tuning parameters based on real-time feedback.

Implementing Parameter Management in ROS2

Let's dive into how to implement both static and dynamic parameters in a ROS2 node using Python.

Step 1: Creating a Node with Parameters

1. **Navigate to Your Package Directory:**

bash

```
cd ~/ros2_ws/src/hello_world/hello_world
```

2. **Create parameter_node.py:**

python

```python
import rclpy
from rclpy.node import Node

class ParameterNode(Node):
    def __init__(self):
        super().__init__('parameter_node')
        # Declare parameters with default values
```

```
        self.declare_parameter('robot_name',
'Robo1')
        self.declare_parameter('max_speed', 1.0)

self.declare_parameter('sensor_threshold', 0.5)

        # Get parameter values
        self.robot_name =
self.get_parameter('robot_name').value
        self.max_speed =
self.get_parameter('max_speed').value
        self.sensor_threshold =
self.get_parameter('sensor_threshold').value

        self.get_logger().info(f'Robot Name:
{self.robot_name}')
        self.get_logger().info(f'Max Speed:
{self.max_speed}')
        self.get_logger().info(f'Sensor
Threshold: {self.sensor_threshold}')

        # Set up a timer to periodically log
parameters
        timer_period = 5.0  # seconds
        self.timer =
self.create_timer(timer_period,
self.timer_callback)
```

```
    # Add callback for parameter changes

self.add_on_set_parameters_callback(self.parameter_callback)

    def timer_callback(self):
        self.get_logger().info(f'Current Parameters - Name: {self.robot_name}, Speed: {self.max_speed}, Threshold: {self.sensor_threshold}')

    def parameter_callback(self, params):
        for param in params:
            if param.name == 'robot_name' and param.type_ == param.TYPE_STRING:
                self.robot_name = param.value
                self.get_logger().info(f'Robot name changed to: {self.robot_name}')
            elif param.name == 'max_speed' and param.type_ == param.TYPE_DOUBLE:
                self.max_speed = param.value
                self.get_logger().info(f'Max speed updated to: {self.max_speed}')
            elif param.name == 'sensor_threshold' and param.type_ == param.TYPE_DOUBLE:
                self.sensor_threshold = param.value
```

[96]

```
        self.get_logger().info(f'Sensor
threshold adjusted to: {self.sensor_threshold}')
        return
rclpy.parameter.SetParametersResult(successful=Tr
ue)


def main(args=None):
    rclpy.init(args=args)
    node = ParameterNode()
    try:
        rclpy.spin(node)
    except KeyboardInterrupt:
        pass
    node.destroy_node()
    rclpy.shutdown()


if __name__ == '__main__':
    main()
```

- o **Explanation:**
  - **Parameter Declaration:** Uses declare_parameter to define parameters with default values.
  - **Parameter Retrieval:** Fetches parameter values using get_parameter.
  - **Timer Callback:** Periodically logs current parameter values.

- **Parameter Callback:** Handles dynamic parameter updates, allowing parameters to be changed at runtime.

3. **Update setup.py:**

Add the parameter node to console_scripts:

python

```python
entry_points={
    'console_scripts': [
        'hello_node =
hello_world.hello_node:main',
        'publisher_node =
hello_world.publisher_node:main',
        'subscriber_node =
hello_world.subscriber_node:main',
        'add_two_ints_service =
hello_world.add_two_ints_service:main',
        'add_two_ints_client =
hello_world.add_two_ints_client:main',
        'lifecycle_node =
hello_world.lifecycle_node:main',
        'parameter_node =
hello_world.parameter_node:main',
    ],
},
```

4. **Make the Script Executable:**

bash

```
chmod +x parameter_node.py
```

Step 2: Building and Running the Parameter Node

1. Navigate to the Workspace Root:

```
bash
```

```
cd ~/ros2_ws
```

2. Build the Package:

```
bash
```

```
colcon build --packages-select hello_world
```

3. Source the Setup File:

```
bash
```

```
source install/setup.bash
```

4. Run the Parameter Node:

```
bash
```

```
ros2 run hello_world parameter_node
```

Expected Output:

```
less
```

```
[INFO] [parameter_node]: Robot Name: Robo1
[INFO] [parameter_node]: Max Speed: 1.0
[INFO] [parameter_node]: Sensor Threshold: 0.5
```

```
[INFO] [parameter_node]: Current Parameters -
Name: Robo1, Speed: 1.0, Threshold: 0.5
```

- The node will log the current parameters every 5 seconds.

Step 3: Modifying Parameters at Runtime

1. **Open a New Terminal and Source the Setup File:**

bash

```
source ~/ros2_ws/install/setup.bash
```

2. **Change the robot_name Parameter:**

bash

```
ros2 param set /parameter_node robot_name "RoboX"
```

Expected Output in Parameter Node Terminal:

css

```
[INFO] [parameter_node]: Robot name changed to:
RoboX
```

3. **Update the max_speed Parameter:**

bash

```
ros2 param set /parameter_node max_speed 2.5
```

Expected Output:

css

```
[INFO] [parameter_node]: Max speed updated to:
2.5
```

4. Adjust the sensor_threshold Parameter:

```bash
ros2 param set /parameter_node sensor_threshold
0.8
```

Expected Output:

```css
[INFO] [parameter_node]: Sensor threshold
adjusted to: 0.8
```

5. Verify Changes:

The timer callback will log the updated parameters every 5 seconds:

```yaml
[INFO] [parameter_node]: Current Parameters -
Name: RoboX, Speed: 2.5, Threshold: 0.8
```

Best Practices for Parameter Management

- **Use Descriptive Names:** Clearly name your parameters to reflect their purpose, aiding in readability and maintainability.

- **Set Reasonable Defaults:** Assign sensible default values to parameters to ensure nodes operate correctly even if parameters aren't explicitly set.

- **Validate Parameters:** Implement checks in your parameter callbacks to ensure values fall within acceptable ranges, preventing unintended behaviors.

- **Document Parameters:** Maintain documentation for your parameters, detailing their purpose, acceptable values, and impact on node behavior.

- **Leverage Parameter Files:** Use YAML or JSON files to manage parameters systematically, especially for complex systems with numerous parameters.

Diagram 2: Parameter Server Interaction

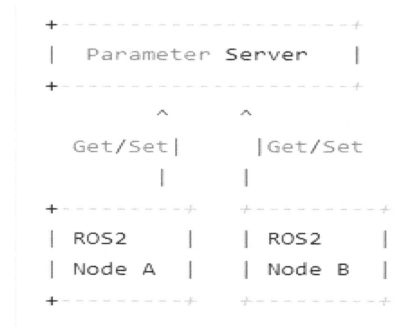

```
+- - - - - - - - - - - - - - - - - - - - +
|   Parameter  Server     |
+- - - - - - - - - - - - - - - - - - - - +

          ^               ^
    Get/Set|          |Get/Set
          |              |
+- - - - - - - - - +    +- - - - - - - - - +
| ROS2      |    | ROS2      |
| Node  A   |    | Node  B   |
+- - - - - - - - - +    +- - - - - - - - - +
```

Description: This diagram illustrates the interaction between nodes and the parameter server in ROS2. It showcases how nodes declare, get, set, and update parameters, highlighting the flow of parameter values and the roles of different components in managing these configurations.

Logging and Debugging

Effective Debugging Techniques in ROS2

Building complex robotic systems inevitably involves encountering and resolving issues. **Logging and Debugging** are essential skills for identifying problems, understanding system behavior, and ensuring smooth operations. ROS2 provides robust tools and practices to aid in effective debugging, making it easier to maintain and optimize your robotic applications.

Importance of Logging and Debugging

- **Issue Identification:** Quickly locate and understand problems within your nodes and communication flows.

- **System Monitoring:** Continuously track the performance and status of your robotic system.

- **Performance Optimization:** Analyze logs to identify bottlenecks and optimize resource usage.

- **Reliability:** Ensure your robotic system operates consistently and predictably by proactively addressing issues.

Implementing Logging in ROS2

Logging is the process of recording messages generated by nodes to provide insights into their operations. ROS2 offers a flexible logging system that supports different log levels and outputs.

Log Levels in ROS2

ROS2 categorizes log messages into different levels based on their severity:

1. **DEBUG:** Detailed information, typically of interest only when diagnosing problems.

2. **INFO:** Confirmation that things are working as expected.

3. **WARN:** Indication that something unexpected happened, but the system can continue.

4. **ERROR:** Serious issues that prevent a node from performing its intended function.

5. **FATAL:** Severe errors causing node termination.

Using the ROS2 Logging API

Let's enhance our previous nodes with logging to better understand their behavior and aid in debugging.

1. Enhancing the Publisher Node with Logging:

```python

import rclpy
from rclpy.node import Node
from std_msgs.msg import String


class PublisherNode(Node):
    def __init__(self):
        super().__init__('publisher_node')
        self.publisher_ =
self.create_publisher(String, 'chatter', 10)
        timer_period = 1.0   # seconds
        self.timer =
self.create_timer(timer_period,
self.timer_callback)
        self.i = 0


    def timer_callback(self):
        msg = String()
        msg.data = f'Hello, ROS2! Count:
{self.i}'
        self.publisher_.publish(msg)
        self.get_logger().info(f'Publishing:
"{msg.data}"')
        self.i += 1


def main(args=None):
```

```
    rclpy.init(args=args)
    node = PublisherNode()
    try:
        rclpy.spin(node)
    except KeyboardInterrupt:
        pass
    node.destroy_node()
    rclpy.shutdown()


if __name__ == '__main__':
    main()
```

- Explanation: The get_logger().info method logs informational messages each time a message is published.

2. **Enhancing the Subscriber Node with Logging:**

python

```
import rclpy
from rclpy.node import Node
from std_msgs.msg import String


class SubscriberNode(Node):
    def __init__(self):
        super().__init__('subscriber_node')
        self.subscription =
self.create_subscription(
            String,
```

```
        'chatter',
        self.listener_callback,
        10)
    self.subscription  # prevent unused
variable warning

    def listener_callback(self, msg):
        self.get_logger().info(f'Received:
"{msg.data}"')


def main(args=None):
    rclpy.init(args=args)
    node = SubscriberNode()
    try:
        rclpy.spin(node)
    except KeyboardInterrupt:
        pass
    node.destroy_node()
    rclpy.shutdown()


if __name__ == '__main__':
    main()
```

- o **Explanation:** The subscriber node logs every message it receives, providing real-time feedback on communication.

Configuring Logging Output

ROS2 allows you to configure the logging output, directing logs to various destinations and setting the verbosity level.

1. **Setting Log Levels at Runtime:**

You can control the verbosity of log messages using environment variables or command-line arguments.

- **Using Environment Variables:**

bash

```
export RCL_LOG_LEVEL=DEBUG
```

- **Using Command-Line Arguments:**

bash

```
ros2 run hello_world publisher_node --ros-args --log-level DEBUG
```

2. **Redirecting Logs to Files:**

To persist logs for later analysis, redirect them to a file.

bash

```
ros2 run hello_world publisher_node > publisher_log.txt 2>&1
```

- **Explanation:** This command directs both standard output and error streams to publisher_log.txt.

Best Practices for Logging

- **Use Appropriate Log Levels:** Choose the correct log level to avoid cluttering logs with unnecessary information. Use DEBUG for detailed troubleshooting, INFO for general status updates, WARN for potential issues, and ERROR for critical failures.

- **Consistent Logging:** Maintain consistent logging practices across all nodes to ensure uniformity and ease of analysis.

- **Meaningful Messages:** Craft clear and descriptive log messages that convey the necessary information without ambiguity.

- **Avoid Sensitive Information:** Ensure logs do not contain sensitive data that could pose security risks.

Debugging Techniques in ROS2

Debugging is the systematic process of identifying, analyzing, and resolving issues within your robotic system. ROS2 provides several tools and methodologies to streamline this process, enabling you to maintain and optimize your applications effectively.

Common Debugging Challenges in ROS2

1. **Silent Failures:** Nodes may fail without providing explicit error messages.

2. **Communication Issues:** Problems in message passing between nodes can disrupt operations.

3. **Resource Leaks:** Improper resource management can lead to degraded performance over time.

4. **Concurrency Issues:** Simultaneous operations may cause unexpected behaviors or conflicts.

Effective Debugging Techniques

1. **Utilize ROS2 Logging:**

   - Leverage the logging system to trace node operations and identify where issues occur.

   - Adjust log levels to gain more detailed insights when necessary.

2. **Use ros2 topic Commands:**

   - **List Topics:**

bash

```
ros2 topic list
```

   - **Echo Topic Messages:**

bash

```
ros2 topic echo /chatter
```

   - **Monitor Topic Info:**

bash

```
ros2 topic info /chatter
```

- o **Explanation:** These commands help verify if topics are active, monitor message flows, and inspect the publishers/subscribers associated with a topic.

3. **Employ ros2 node Commands:**

```
List Nodes:
bash
```

```
ros2 node list
```

- o **Get Node Info:**

```
bash
```

```
ros2 node info /publisher_node
```

- o **Explanation:** These commands provide information about active nodes, their subscriptions, publications, and services, aiding in diagnosing communication issues.

4. **Use ROS2 Tools like rviz2:**

- o **RViz2:** A 3D visualization tool for ROS2 that allows you to visualize sensor data, robot models, and more.

- o **Usage:**

```
bash
```

```
ros2 run rviz2 rviz2
```

o **Explanation:** Visualizing data can help identify issues related to sensor inputs, robot states, and environment interactions.

5. **Implement Assertions and Checks in Code:**

   o **Example:**

python

assert self.publisher_ is not None, 'Publisher not initialized!'

   o **Explanation:** Assertions can catch unexpected states or missing components early in the development process.

6. **Use Debuggers like gdb or IDE Integrated Debuggers:**

   o **gdb:** A powerful debugger for C/C++ nodes.

   o **IDE Debuggers:** Most modern IDEs like Visual Studio Code and PyCharm offer integrated debugging tools for Python.

   o **Usage in VS Code:**

      ▪ Set breakpoints in your Python scripts.

      ▪ Use the debug panel to start a debugging session, inspect variables, and step through code.

7. **Monitor System Resources:**

   o **Commands:**

```bash
top
htop
```

  o **Explanation:** Monitor CPU and memory usage to identify resource bottlenecks or leaks.

8. **Leverage ros2 lifecycle Commands:**

  o **Manage Node States:**

```bash
ros2 lifecycle set /lifecycle_example_node
deactivate
```

  o **Explanation:** Control node states to test transitions and ensure nodes handle state changes gracefully.

Debugging Example: Resolving a Publisher-Subscriber Issue

Let's walk through a common debugging scenario where the subscriber node isn't receiving messages from the publisher node.

1. **Verify Nodes are Running:**

```bash
ros2 node list
```

Expected Output:

```bash
```

```
/publisher_node
/subscriber_node
```

- o **If Nodes are Missing:** Ensure both nodes are running without errors.

2. **Check Topic Existence:**

```
bash
```

```
ros2 topic list
```

Expected Output:

```
bash
```

```
/chatter
```

- o **If Topic is Missing:** Ensure the publisher node is correctly publishing to the /chatter topic.

3. **Inspect Topic Info:**

```
bash
```

```
ros2 topic info /chatter
```

Expected Output:

```
vbnet
```

Type: std_msgs/msg/String

Publishers:

/publisher_node

Subscribers:

/subscriber_node

- o **If No Subscribers:** Confirm that the subscriber node is correctly subscribing to the /chatter topic.

4. **Echo Topic Messages:**

```bash
ros2 topic echo /chatter
```

- o **Expected Output:**

```yaml
data: "Hello, ROS2! Count: 0"
---
data: "Hello, ROS2! Count: 1"
---
```

- o **If No Messages:** Investigate the publisher node's timer and ensure it's actively publishing messages.

5. **Review Logs:**

Check both publisher and subscriber node logs for any error messages or warnings.

```bash
ros2 run hello_world publisher_node
ros2 run hello_world subscriber_node
```

- ○ **Look for Errors:** Identify any issues related to topic creation, message publishing, or subscription failures.

6. **Use RViz2 for Visualization:**

```bash
ros2 run rviz2 rviz2
```

- ○ **Add a String Display:** Visualize the messages being published to the /chatter topic.

- ○ **Explanation:** If messages appear in RViz2 but not in the subscriber node, the issue might lie within the subscriber's callback implementation.

7. **Inspect Code for Errors:**

- ○ **Publisher Node:** Ensure the publisher is correctly initializing and publishing messages.

- ○ **Subscriber Node:** Verify that the subscriber's callback is correctly processing incoming messages.

8. **Restart Nodes:**

Sometimes, restarting nodes can resolve transient issues.

```bash
ros2 run hello_world publisher_node
ros2 run hello_world subscriber_node
```

- o **Explanation:** Reinitializing nodes can reset communication channels and resolve connection issues.

Diagram 3: ROS2 Logging Framework

```
+- - - - - - - - - - - - - - - - - - - - - - - - - +
|           ROS2 Logging API             |
|    (rclpy, rclcpp logging methods)|
+- - - - - - - - - - - - +- - - - - - - - - - - - +
                        |
                        v
    +- - - - - - - - - - - - - - - - - - - - +
    |        Log Message Format      |
    |     (Timestamp, Log Level,  |
    |      Node Name, Message)      |
    +- - - - - - - - - - - - - - - - - - - - +
                        |
                        v
    +- - - - - - - - - - - - - - - - - - - - +
    |      Logging Sinks/Targets  |
    +- - - - - - - - - - - - - - - - - - - - +
              /                    \
             /                      \
            v                        v
+- - - - - - - - - - - +    +- - - - - - - - - - - - - +
| Console Sink |    |   File Sink       |
|    (STDOUT)   |    |   (Log Files,     |
|               |    |    with Rotation)|
+- - - - - - - - - - - +    +- - - - - - - - - - - - - +
```

Description: This diagram visualizes the ROS2 logging framework, illustrating how log messages flow from nodes to various outputs based on log levels. It highlights the different log levels (DEBUG, INFO, WARN, ERROR, FATAL) and their destinations (console, files), demonstrating how ROS2 manages and categorizes log information to aid in debugging and system monitoring.

Summary

In **Chapter 4: Advanced ROS2 Concepts**, we've explored the sophisticated mechanisms that ensure your robotic systems are robust, adaptable, and efficient. Here's a recap of what we've covered:

1. **Lifecycle Management:**

   - **Understanding Node Lifecycles:** Learned about the states (Inactive, Activating, Active, Deactivating, Finalized) and transitions that govern node behavior.

   - **Implementing Managed Nodes:** Created a lifecycle-managed node in Python, enabling controlled state transitions and ensuring predictable operations.

2. **Parameter Management:**

   - **Dynamic and Static Parameters:** Explored the flexibility of configuring node parameters both at initialization and runtime.

   - **Implementing Parameter Nodes:** Developed a node that handles both static and dynamic parameters, allowing real-time adjustments to node behavior.

3. **Logging and Debugging:**

   o **ROS2 Logging System:** Utilized ROS2's logging capabilities to monitor node operations, adjust verbosity levels, and direct logs to various outputs.

   o **Effective Debugging Techniques:** Employed tools like ros2 topic, ros2 node commands, RViz2, and integrated debuggers to identify and resolve issues within the ROS2 ecosystem.

4. **Visual Diagrams:**

   o Provided conceptual diagrams to visualize node lifecycles, parameter interactions, and communication models, reinforcing the understanding of advanced ROS2 concepts.

With these advanced concepts under your belt, you're now prepared to build more resilient and adaptable robotic systems. As you continue your journey, these skills will enable you to manage complex node interactions, optimize system performance, and maintain the reliability of your autonomous robots.

Next Steps:

With a solid foundation in advanced ROS2 concepts, you're ready to enhance your Python programming skills for robotics. In the upcoming chapter, **Python Programming for Robotics**, we'll dive into object-oriented programming, asynchronous operations, and integrating machine learning libraries with ROS2. These skills will empower you to create intelligent and responsive robotic behaviors, taking your autonomous systems to the next level.

Final Encouragement

Embarking on the journey of mastering advanced ROS2 concepts is both challenging and rewarding. You've taken a significant step towards building intelligent, resilient, and adaptable robotic systems that can transform industries and enhance our daily lives. Remember, every expert was once a beginner, and every complex system starts with understanding its core components.

As you move forward, embrace the challenges and continue experimenting with the concepts you've learned. The world of autonomous robotics is vast and ever-evolving, offering endless opportunities for innovation and growth. Stay curious, stay persistent, and most importantly, enjoy the process of creating and refining your robotic creations.

Happy building!

Chapter 5: Python Programming for Robotics

Welcome to the pivotal chapter of your robotics journey! As you delve deeper into the world of autonomous systems, mastering Python programming becomes essential. Python's versatility, combined with its extensive library ecosystem, makes it an ideal choice for developing sophisticated robotic applications. In this chapter, we'll explore **Object-Oriented Programming (OOP)** in Python, **Asynchronous Programming** using asyncio, and the integration of **Machine Learning Libraries** like TensorFlow, PyTorch, and scikit-learn with ROS2. By the end of this chapter, you'll be equipped with the skills to write efficient, scalable, and intelligent robotic software.

Object-Oriented Programming in Python

Classes, Inheritance, and Polymorphism

Have you ever tried organizing a cluttered toolbox without labels? Just as labels help you find the right tool quickly, **Object-Oriented Programming (OOP)** helps structure your code, making it more organized, reusable, and maintainable. Let's unravel the core concepts of OOP in Python and understand how they empower you to build robust robotic applications.

What is Object-Oriented Programming?

Object-Oriented Programming (OOP) is a programming paradigm that organizes software design around **objects** rather than actions and data rather than logic. An object can be thought of as a self-contained component that consists of both data and procedures to manipulate that data.

Core Concepts of OOP

1. **Classes and Objects**

   o **Class:** A blueprint for creating objects. It defines a set of attributes and methods that the created objects will have.

   o **Object:** An instance of a class. It represents a specific entity with actual values.

Analogy: Think of a class as a blueprint for a car. The object is the actual car built from that blueprint.

python

```python
class Robot:
    def __init__(self, name, max_speed):
        self.name = name
        self.max_speed = max_speed

    def move(self):
```

```
        print(f"{self.name} is moving at
{self.max_speed} m/s.")


# Creating an object of the Robot class
robo1 = Robot("RoboX", 2.5)
robo1.move()
# Output: RoboX is moving at 2.5 m/s.
```

2. Inheritance

- o **Definition:** A mechanism where a new class inherits attributes and methods from an existing class.

- o **Purpose:** Promotes code reusability and establishes a natural hierarchy between classes.

Analogy: Consider a generic vehicle class and a specific car class. The car inherits common attributes like wheels and engine from the vehicle.

python

```
class Vehicle:
    def __init__(self, name, wheels):
        self.name = name
        self.wheels = wheels


    def move(self):
        print(f"{self.name} is moving with
{self.wheels} wheels.")
```

```
class Car(Vehicle):
    def __init__(self, name, wheels, max_speed):
        super().__init__(name, wheels)
        self.max_speed = max_speed

    def move(self):
        print(f"{self.name} is driving at
{self.max_speed} km/h with {self.wheels}
wheels.")


# Creating an object of the Car class
car1 = Car("Speedster", 4, 180)
car1.move()
# Output: Speedster is driving at 180 km/h with 4
wheels.
```

3. **Polymorphism**

  o **Definition:** The ability to present the same interface for different underlying forms (data types).

  o **Purpose:** Enhances flexibility and integration of different classes.

Analogy: Different musicians playing the same musical instrument (e.g., violin) but producing unique sounds.

```
python


class Dog:
    def speak(self):
```

```
        print("Woof!")

class Cat:
    def speak(self):
        print("Meow!")

def animal_sound(animal):
    animal.speak()

dog = Dog()
cat = Cat()

animal_sound(dog)   # Output: Woof!
animal_sound(cat)   # Output: Meow!
```

Benefits of OOP in Robotics

- **Modularity:** Code is organized into manageable, self-contained units (classes), making it easier to understand and maintain.

- **Reusability:** Inheritance allows for the reuse of existing code, reducing redundancy.

- **Scalability:** Polymorphism enables the integration of diverse components, facilitating the expansion of robotic systems.

- **Maintainability:** Clear structure and encapsulation make it easier to locate and fix bugs.

Diagram 1: OOP Concepts in Python

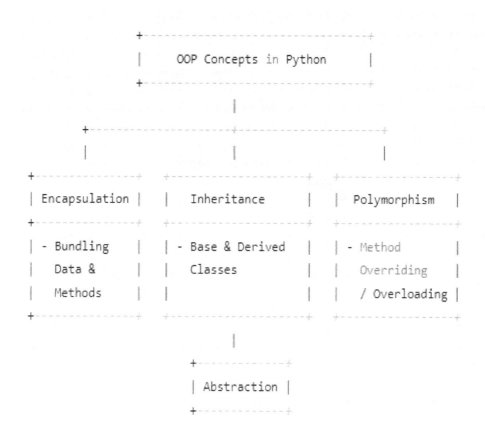

Description: This diagram visually represents the core concepts of Object-Oriented Programming in Python. It showcases how classes serve as blueprints for objects, illustrates inheritance hierarchies, and demonstrates polymorphism through method overriding.

Asynchronous Programming

Asyncio and Its Role in Robotics

Have you ever tried juggling multiple tasks simultaneously without dropping any? **Asynchronous Programming** in Python allows you to manage multiple operations concurrently, ensuring your robotic applications remain responsive and efficient. Let's explore how asyncio, Python's built-in library for asynchronous programming, plays a pivotal role in robotics.

What is Asynchronous Programming?

Asynchronous Programming is a programming paradigm that allows multiple tasks to run concurrently without waiting for each other to complete. It enhances the efficiency of applications by utilizing time effectively, especially when dealing with I/O-bound operations.

Why Asynchronous Programming in Robotics?

Robotic systems often involve tasks that require waiting, such as sensor data acquisition, communication with other devices, and processing complex algorithms. Asynchronous programming allows these tasks to run concurrently, preventing your robot from becoming unresponsive or sluggish.

Analogy: Imagine a restaurant kitchen where the chef can simultaneously prepare multiple dishes without waiting for each to finish one by one. This parallelism ensures efficient use of time and resources.

Introduction to Asyncio

Asyncio is Python's standard library for writing concurrent code using the async and await syntax. It provides a foundation for building asynchronous applications, making it ideal for robotics where multiple tasks need to run in parallel.

Core Concepts of Asyncio

1. **Coroutines**

    o **Definition:** Special functions defined with async def that can pause and resume their execution.

    o **Usage:** Encapsulate asynchronous tasks.

python

```python
import asyncio

async def greet(name):
    await asyncio.sleep(1)
    print(f"Hello, {name}!")

asyncio.run(greet("RoboX"))
# Output (after 1 second): Hello, RoboX!
```

2. Event Loop

- o **Definition:** The core of every asyncio application. It manages and dispatches all events and coroutines.

- o **Usage:** Runs asynchronous tasks and callbacks.

```python

import asyncio

async def greet(name):
    await asyncio.sleep(1)
    print(f"Hello, {name}!")

async def main():
    await asyncio.gather(
        greet("RoboX"),
        greet("RoboY"),
        greet("RoboZ")
    )

asyncio.run(main())
# Output (after 1 second):
# Hello, RoboX!
# Hello, RoboY!
# Hello, RoboZ!
```

3. Tasks

- Definition: Wrappers for coroutines that schedule their execution within the event loop.

- Usage: Manage multiple coroutines concurrently.

```python
import asyncio

async def task1():
    await asyncio.sleep(2)
    print("Task 1 completed")

async def task2():
    await asyncio.sleep(1)
    print("Task 2 completed")

async def main():
    t1 = asyncio.create_task(task1())
    t2 = asyncio.create_task(task2())
    await t1
    await t2

asyncio.run(main())
# Output (after 1 second): Task 2 completed
# Output (after 2 seconds): Task 1 completed
```

Implementing Asyncio in ROS2

ROS2 nodes often need to handle multiple tasks such as sensor data processing, communication, and control commands. Integrating asyncio with ROS2 allows these tasks to run concurrently, enhancing the system's efficiency and responsiveness.

Example: Asynchronous Sensor Data Acquisition

Let's create a ROS2 node that asynchronously reads sensor data while performing other tasks.

1. **Create async_sensor_node.py:**

```python

import rclpy
from rclpy.node import Node
from std_msgs.msg import Float32
import asyncio


class AsyncSensorNode(Node):
    def __init__(self):
        super().__init__('async_sensor_node')
        self.publisher_ =
self.create_publisher(Float32, 'sensor_data', 10)
        self.get_logger().info('AsyncSensorNode has been started.')
        self.loop = asyncio.get_event_loop()
```

```python
        self.loop.create_task(self.publish_sensor_data())

    async def publish_sensor_data(self):
        while rclpy.ok():
            sensor_value = self.read_sensor()
            msg = Float32()
            msg.data = sensor_value
            self.publisher_.publish(msg)
            self.get_logger().info(f'Published
sensor data: {sensor_value}')
            await asyncio.sleep(1)  # Simulate
sensor reading delay

    def read_sensor(self):
        # Simulate reading sensor data
        import random
        return random.uniform(0.0, 100.0)

def main(args=None):
    rclpy.init(args=args)
    node = AsyncSensorNode()
    try:
        rclpy.spin(node)
    except KeyboardInterrupt:
        pass
    node.destroy_node()
    rclpy.shutdown()
```

```
if __name__ == '__main__':
    main()
```

- o **Explanation:**
  - **Asynchronous Task:** publish_sensor_data is an asynchronous coroutine that publishes sensor data every second without blocking the node.
  - **Event Loop:** Integrates asyncio's event loop with ROS2's spinning mechanism to manage asynchronous tasks seamlessly.

2. **Update setup.py:**

Add the async sensor node to console_scripts:

```python
entry_points={
    'console_scripts': [
        'hello_node =
hello_world.hello_node:main',
        'publisher_node =
hello_world.publisher_node:main',
        'subscriber_node =
hello_world.subscriber_node:main',
        'add_two_ints_service =
hello_world.add_two_ints_service:main',
```

```
        'add_two_ints_client =
hello_world.add_two_ints_client:main',
        'lifecycle_node =
hello_world.lifecycle_node:main',
        'parameter_node =
hello_world.parameter_node:main',
        'async_sensor_node =
hello_world.async_sensor_node:main',
    ],
},
```

3. **Make the Script Executable:**

```bash
bash
```

```
chmod +x async_sensor_node.py
```

4. **Build and Source the Workspace:**

```bash
bash
```

```
cd ~/ros2_ws
colcon build --packages-select hello_world
source install/setup.bash
```

5. **Run the Async Sensor Node:**

```bash
bash
```

```
ros2 run hello_world async_sensor_node
```

Expected Output:

```
less
```

```
[INFO] [async_sensor_node]: AsyncSensorNode has
been started.
[INFO] [async_sensor_node]: Published sensor
data: 42.7
[INFO] [async_sensor_node]: Published sensor
data: 76.3
...
```

○ The node publishes random sensor data every second without blocking other operations.

Best Practices for Asynchronous Programming

- **Avoid Blocking Calls:** Ensure that any long-running operations are handled asynchronously to prevent blocking the event loop.

- **Handle Exceptions Gracefully:** Implement proper error handling within asynchronous tasks to prevent unexpected crashes.

- **Manage Task Lifecycles:** Ensure that asynchronous tasks are properly managed and terminated when the node shuts down.

- **Use asyncio.gather for Concurrency:** When running multiple coroutines, use asyncio.gather to manage them efficiently.

Diagram 2: Asyncio Event Loop

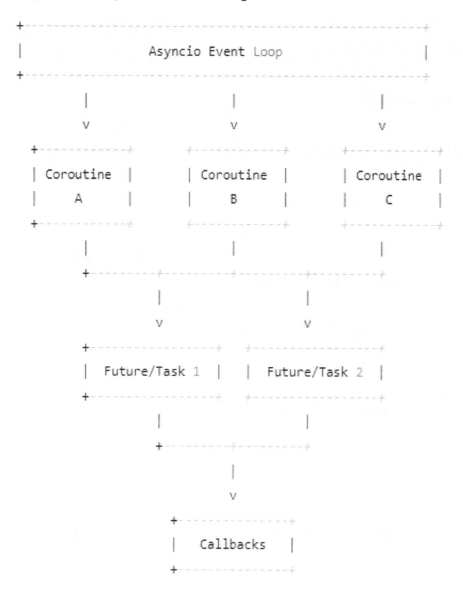

Description: This diagram illustrates the structure and flow of Python's asyncio event loop. It highlights how coroutines, tasks, and the event loop interact to manage asynchronous operations, enabling concurrent execution without blocking the main thread.

Integrating Machine Learning Libraries

Using TensorFlow, PyTorch, and scikit-learn with ROS2

Imagine teaching a robot to recognize objects, make decisions based on data, or navigate complex environments autonomously. **Machine Learning (ML)** is the key to unlocking such intelligent behaviors. Integrating ML libraries like **TensorFlow, PyTorch**, and **scikit-learn** with ROS2 empowers your robots with advanced capabilities, enabling them to learn, adapt, and perform complex tasks with minimal human intervention.

Why Integrate Machine Learning with ROS2?

- **Enhanced Perception:** Enable robots to interpret sensor data, recognize objects, and understand their environment.

- **Intelligent Decision-Making:** Allow robots to make informed decisions based on learned patterns and data analysis.

- **Autonomous Navigation:** Facilitate navigation in dynamic and unstructured environments by learning from past experiences.

- **Predictive Maintenance:** Anticipate system failures and perform maintenance tasks proactively.

Overview of Key Machine Learning Libraries

1. TensorFlow

   o **Description:** An open-source ML library developed by Google, widely used for building and deploying machine learning models.

   o **Use Cases:** Deep learning, neural networks, computer vision, natural language processing.

2. PyTorch

   o **Description:** An open-source ML library developed by Facebook's AI Research lab, known for its dynamic computation graph and ease of use.

   o **Use Cases:** Deep learning, research experiments, rapid prototyping, computer vision.

3. scikit-learn

   o **Description:** A versatile ML library for Python, providing simple and efficient tools for data mining and data analysis.

o **Use Cases:** Classification, regression, clustering, dimensionality reduction.

Integrating TensorFlow with ROS2

Let's explore how to integrate **TensorFlow** with ROS2 to enable object recognition in a robotic system.

Example: Object Recognition with TensorFlow and ROS2

1. **Prerequisites:**

   o **TensorFlow Installation:** Ensure TensorFlow is installed in your Python environment.

bash

```
pip install tensorflow
```

   o **Pre-trained Model:** Use a pre-trained model like **MobileNet** for object detection.

2. **Create object_recognition_node.py:**

python

```python
import rclpy
from rclpy.node import Node
from sensor_msgs.msg import Image
from cv_bridge import CvBridge
import tensorflow as tf
import numpy as np
import cv2
```

```python
class ObjectRecognitionNode(Node):
    def __init__(self):

super().__init__('object_recognition_node')
        self.subscription =
self.create_subscription(
            Image,
            'camera/image',
            self.listener_callback,
            10)
        self.subscription  # prevent unused
variable warning
        self.bridge = CvBridge()
        self.model = self.load_model()

self.get_logger().info('ObjectRecognitionNode has
been started.')

    def load_model(self):
        # Load a pre-trained TensorFlow model
(e.g., MobileNet)
        model =
tf.keras.applications.MobileNetV2(weights='imagen
et', include_top=True)
        self.get_logger().info('TensorFlow model
loaded successfully.')
        return model
```

```python
    def preprocess_image(self, cv_image):
        # Preprocess the image for the model
        img = cv2.resize(cv_image, (224, 224))
        img =
tf.keras.applications.mobilenet_v2.preprocess_inp
ut(img)
        img = np.expand_dims(img, axis=0)
        return img


    def listener_callback(self, msg):
        # Convert ROS Image message to OpenCV
image
        cv_image = self.bridge.imgmsg_to_cv2(msg,
desired_encoding='bgr8')
        processed_image =
self.preprocess_image(cv_image)
        predictions =
self.model.predict(processed_image)
        decoded_predictions =
tf.keras.applications.mobilenet_v2.decode_predict
ions(predictions, top=3)[0]
        for i, (imagenet_id, label, score) in
enumerate(decoded_predictions):
            self.get_logger().info(f"Prediction
{i+1}: {label} ({score*100:.2f}%)")

def main(args=None):
    rclpy.init(args=args)
```

```
node = ObjectRecognitionNode()
try:
    rclpy.spin(node)
except KeyboardInterrupt:
    pass
node.destroy_node()
rclpy.shutdown()


if __name__ == '__main__':
    main()
```

- o **Explanation:**

  - **TensorFlow Model Loading:** Loads a pre-trained MobileNetV2 model for object recognition.

  - **Image Preprocessing:** Resizes and preprocesses incoming images to match the model's input requirements.

  - **Prediction:** Runs inference on the processed image and decodes the top-3 predictions.

  - **Logging:** Outputs the predictions with labels and confidence scores.

3. **Update setup.py:**

Add the object recognition node to console_scripts:

```python
```

```
entry_points={
    'console_scripts': [
        'hello_node =
hello_world.hello_node:main',
        'publisher_node =
hello_world.publisher_node:main',
        'subscriber_node =
hello_world.subscriber_node:main',
        'add_two_ints_service =
hello_world.add_two_ints_service:main',
        'add_two_ints_client =
hello_world.add_two_ints_client:main',
        'lifecycle_node =
hello_world.lifecycle_node:main',
        'parameter_node =
hello_world.parameter_node:main',
        'async_sensor_node =
hello_world.async_sensor_node:main',
        'object_recognition_node =
hello_world.object_recognition_node:main',
    ],
},
```

4. Make the Script Executable:

```bash

chmod +x object_recognition_node.py
```

5. Build and Source the Workspace:

```
bash
```

```
cd ~/ros2_ws
colcon build --packages-select hello_world
source install/setup.bash
```

6. **Run the Object Recognition Node:**

```
bash
```

```
ros2 run hello_world object_recognition_node
```

Expected Output:

```
less
```

```
[INFO] [object_recognition_node]: TensorFlow
model loaded successfully.
[INFO] [object_recognition_node]:
ObjectRecognitionNode has been started.
[INFO] [object_recognition_node]: Prediction 1:
Labrador_retriever (95.23%)
[INFO] [object_recognition_node]: Prediction 2:
golden_retriever (2.56%)
[INFO] [object_recognition_node]: Prediction 3:
beagle (1.21%)
```

- o The node processes incoming images, performs object recognition, and logs the top-3 predictions.

Integrating PyTorch with ROS2

PyTorch offers dynamic computation graphs and is favored for research and rapid prototyping. Let's integrate PyTorch with ROS2 for a simple classification task.

Example: Image Classification with PyTorch and ROS2

1. **Prerequisites:**

   o **PyTorch Installation:**

bash

```bash
pip install torch torchvision
```

   o **Pre-trained Model:** Use a pre-trained ResNet model for image classification.

2. **Create image_classification_node.py:**

python

```python
import rclpy
from rclpy.node import Node
from sensor_msgs.msg import Image
from cv_bridge import CvBridge
import torch
import torchvision.transforms as transforms
from PIL import Image as PILImage

class ImageClassificationNode(Node):
    def __init__(self):
```

```python
super().__init__('image_classification_node')
        self.subscription =
self.create_subscription(
            Image,
            'camera/image',
            self.listener_callback,
            10)
        self.subscription  # prevent unused
variable warning
        self.bridge = CvBridge()
        self.model = self.load_model()
        self.transform = transforms.Compose([
            transforms.Resize(256),
            transforms.CenterCrop(224),
            transforms.ToTensor(),
            transforms.Normalize(
                mean=[0.485, 0.456, 0.406],
                std=[0.229, 0.224, 0.225]
            )
        ])


self.get_logger().info('ImageClassificationNode
has been started.')

    def load_model(self):
        # Load a pre-trained ResNet model
```

```python
        model =
torch.hub.load('pytorch/vision:v0.10.0',
'resnet18', pretrained=True)
        model.eval()
        self.get_logger().info('PyTorch model
loaded successfully.')
        return model


    def listener_callback(self, msg):
        # Convert ROS Image message to OpenCV
image
        cv_image = self.bridge.imgmsg_to_cv2(msg,
desired_encoding='bgr8')
        pil_image = PILImage.fromarray(cv_image)
        input_tensor = self.transform(pil_image)
        input_batch = input_tensor.unsqueeze(0)
# Create a mini-batch as expected by the model

        with torch.no_grad():
            output = self.model(input_batch)
        _, predicted = torch.max(output, 1)
        self.get_logger().info(f'Predicted Class
ID: {predicted.item()}')

def main(args=None):
    rclpy.init(args=args)
    node = ImageClassificationNode()
    try:
```

```
    rclpy.spin(node)
except KeyboardInterrupt:
    pass
node.destroy_node()
rclpy.shutdown()


if __name__ == '__main__':
    main()
```

- ○ **Explanation:**

  - ▪ **PyTorch Model Loading:** Loads a pre-trained ResNet18 model for image classification.

  - ▪ **Image Preprocessing:** Transforms incoming images to match the model's input requirements.

  - ▪ **Prediction:** Runs inference on the processed image and logs the predicted class ID.

3. Update setup.py:

Add the image classification node to console_scripts:

```python


entry_points={
    'console_scripts': [
        'hello_node =
hello_world.hello_node:main',
```

```
        'publisher_node =
hello_world.publisher_node:main',
        'subscriber_node =
hello_world.subscriber_node:main',
        'add_two_ints_service =
hello_world.add_two_ints_service:main',
        'add_two_ints_client =
hello_world.add_two_ints_client:main',
        'lifecycle_node =
hello_world.lifecycle_node:main',
        'parameter_node =
hello_world.parameter_node:main',
        'async_sensor_node =
hello_world.async_sensor_node:main',
        'object_recognition_node =
hello_world.object_recognition_node:main',
        'image_classification_node =
hello_world.image_classification_node:main',
    ],
},
```

4. Make the Script Executable:

bash

```
chmod +x image_classification_node.py
```

5. Build and Source the Workspace:

bash

```
cd ~/ros2_ws
colcon build --packages-select hello_world
source install/setup.bash
```

6. **Run the Image Classification Node:**

```bash
```

```
ros2 run hello_world image_classification_node
```

Expected Output:

```less
```

```
[INFO] [image_classification_node]: PyTorch model
loaded successfully.
[INFO] [image_classification_node]:
ImageClassificationNode has been started.
[INFO] [image_classification_node]: Predicted
Class ID: 243
[INFO] [image_classification_node]: Predicted
Class ID: 281
...
```

- o The node processes incoming images, classifies them using the PyTorch model, and logs the predicted class IDs.

Integrating scikit-learn with ROS2

scikit-learn is a versatile ML library ideal for data analysis, preprocessing, and implementing traditional machine

learning algorithms. Let's integrate scikit-learn with ROS2 for
a simple clustering task.

Example: Clustering Sensor Data with scikit-learn and ROS2

1. **Prerequisites:**

   o **scikit-learn Installation:**

bash

```
pip install scikit-learn
```

2. **Create sensor_clustering_node.py:**

python

```
import rclpy
from rclpy.node import Node
from std_msgs.msg import Float32MultiArray
from sklearn.cluster import KMeans
import numpy as np

class SensorClusteringNode(Node):
    def __init__(self):

super().__init__('sensor_clustering_node')
        self.subscription =
self.create_subscription(
            Float32MultiArray,
            'sensor_data',
            self.listener_callback,
```

```
        10)
        self.subscription  # prevent unused
variable warning
        self.kmeans = KMeans(n_clusters=2)
        self.data_buffer = []

self.get_logger().info('SensorClusteringNode has
been started.')

    def listener_callback(self, msg):
        # Append incoming data to buffer
        data = msg.data
        self.data_buffer.append(data)
        self.get_logger().info(f'Received sensor
data: {data}')

        # Perform clustering every 10 data points
        if len(self.data_buffer) >= 10:
            self.perform_clustering()

    def perform_clustering(self):
        data = np.array(self.data_buffer)
        self.kmeans.fit(data)
        labels = self.kmeans.labels_
        self.get_logger().info(f'Clustering
Labels: {labels}')
        # Clear the buffer after clustering
        self.data_buffer = []
```

```python
def main(args=None):
    rclpy.init(args=args)
    node = SensorClusteringNode()
    try:
        rclpy.spin(node)
    except KeyboardInterrupt:
        pass
    node.destroy_node()
    rclpy.shutdown()


if __name__ == '__main__':
    main()
```

- o **Explanation:**

    - **KMeans Clustering:** Initializes a KMeans model to cluster sensor data into 2 groups.

    - **Data Buffering:** Collects incoming sensor data and performs clustering after accumulating 10 data points.

    - **Logging:** Outputs the clustering labels for analysis.

3. Update setup.py:

Add the sensor clustering node to console_scripts:

```python
```

```python
entry_points={
```

```
    'console_scripts': [
        'hello_node =
hello_world.hello_node:main',
        'publisher_node =
hello_world.publisher_node:main',
        'subscriber_node =
hello_world.subscriber_node:main',
        'add_two_ints_service =
hello_world.add_two_ints_service:main',
        'add_two_ints_client =
hello_world.add_two_ints_client:main',
        'lifecycle_node =
hello_world.lifecycle_node:main',
        'parameter_node =
hello_world.parameter_node:main',
        'async_sensor_node =
hello_world.async_sensor_node:main',
        'object_recognition_node =
hello_world.object_recognition_node:main',
        'image_classification_node =
hello_world.image_classification_node:main',
        'sensor_clustering_node =
hello_world.sensor_clustering_node:main',
    ],
},
```

4. Make the Script Executable:

```bash
bash
```

```
chmod +x sensor_clustering_node.py
```

5. Build and Source the Workspace:

```bash
```

```
cd ~/ros2_ws
colcon build --packages-select hello_world
source install/setup.bash
```

6. Run the Sensor Clustering Node:

```bash
```

```
ros2 run hello_world sensor_clustering_node
```

Expected Output:

```less
```

```
[INFO] [sensor_clustering_node]:
SensorClusteringNode has been started.
[INFO] [sensor_clustering_node]: Received sensor
data: [23.5, 47.2, 12.3]
...
[INFO] [sensor_clustering_node]: Clustering
Labels: [0 1 0 1 0 1 0 1 0 1]
```

o The node collects sensor data, performs clustering every 10 data points, and logs the clustering results.

Best Practices for Integrating Machine Learning with ROS2

- **Model Optimization:** Optimize ML models for real-time performance to ensure they don't become bottlenecks in your system.

- **Resource Management:** Allocate sufficient computational resources for ML tasks, especially for deep learning models that require significant processing power.

- **Data Handling:** Implement efficient data preprocessing and handling mechanisms to manage large volumes of sensor data.

- **Continuous Learning:** Incorporate mechanisms for model updates and retraining to adapt to new environments and data.

- **Modular Design:** Keep ML components modular, allowing for easy integration, testing, and replacement of models.

Summary

In **Chapter 5: Python Programming for Robotics**, we've explored the essential programming paradigms and tools that empower you to build intelligent and efficient robotic systems. Here's a quick recap of what we've covered:

1. **Object-Oriented Programming (OOP):**

   ○ **Core Concepts:** Classes, inheritance, and polymorphism.

   ○ **Practical Implementation:** Demonstrated how OOP enhances code organization, reusability, and scalability in robotic applications through Python examples.

2. **Asynchronous Programming with Asyncio:**

   ○ **Principles of Asynchronous Programming:** Introduced the concepts of coroutines, event loops, and tasks.

   ○ **Integration with ROS2:** Showcased how to implement asynchronous tasks within ROS2 nodes to handle sensor data acquisition without blocking operations.

3. **Integrating Machine Learning Libraries:**

   ○ **TensorFlow Integration:** Enabled object recognition by integrating a pre-trained TensorFlow model with a ROS2 node.

   ○ **PyTorch Integration:** Demonstrated image classification using a pre-trained PyTorch model within a ROS2 node.

   ○ **scikit-learn Integration:** Illustrated clustering of sensor data using scikit-learn within a ROS2 node.

- ○ **Practical Examples:** Provided hands-on examples that bridge the gap between machine learning models and ROS2's communication infrastructure.

4. **Visual Diagrams:**

   - ○ **OOP Concepts in Python:** Visualized the relationship between classes, objects, inheritance, and polymorphism.

   - ○ **Asyncio Event Loop:** Illustrated the flow and management of asynchronous tasks using asyncio.

   - ○ **ML Integration Workflow:** Outlined the process of integrating machine learning models with ROS2, from data acquisition to decision-making.

With these foundational programming skills, you're now equipped to create sophisticated, intelligent, and responsive robotic systems. By leveraging Python's powerful features and integrating advanced machine learning techniques, you can elevate your robotics projects to new heights, enabling your robots to perform complex tasks autonomously and adaptively.

Next Steps: Building Intelligent Systems

With a solid foundation in Python programming and its application in robotics, you're now ready to take your projects further. In the next chapter, **Building Intelligent Systems**, we'll explore how to integrate various sensors, implement perception algorithms, and develop autonomous navigation capabilities. This will enable your robots to interact intelligently with their environments, paving the way for more complex and autonomous behaviors.

Final Encouragement

You've made significant strides in mastering Python programming for robotics. As you move forward, continue to experiment, explore new libraries, and refine your coding practices. The journey of building intelligent robotic systems is both challenging and rewarding, offering endless opportunities for innovation and growth. Keep pushing the boundaries, stay curious, and embrace the exciting challenges that lie ahead. Your expertise and dedication are the keys to unlocking the full potential of autonomous robotics.

Happy coding!

Chapter 6: Building Intelligent Systems

Welcome to **Chapter 6: Building Intelligent Systems!** You've journeyed through setting up your development environment, grasping the fundamentals of ROS2, and mastering advanced ROS2 concepts. Now, it's time to bring it all together and construct intelligent robotic systems capable of perceiving their environment, making informed decisions, and navigating autonomously. In this chapter, we'll explore **Sensor Integration**, delve into **Perception and Computer Vision**, tackle **Path Planning and Navigation**, and culminate with a hands-on project: **Building a Smart Mobile Robot.** Let's embark on this exciting endeavor!

Sensor Integration

Working with LIDAR, Cameras, and Other Sensors

Have you ever wondered how autonomous vehicles effortlessly navigate through bustling city streets or how drones capture stunning aerial imagery? The secret lies in their ability to **integrate and interpret data from various sensors.** In robotics, **Sensor Integration** is the backbone of creating systems that can perceive and interact with their environment intelligently.

What is Sensor Integration?

Sensor Integration involves combining data from multiple sensors to create a comprehensive understanding of the robot's surroundings. By leveraging different types of sensors, robots can achieve a higher level of accuracy, reliability, and functionality. Common sensors used in robotics include:

- **LIDAR (Light Detection and Ranging):** Measures distances by illuminating targets with laser light and analyzing the reflected light.

- **Cameras:** Capture visual information, enabling tasks like object recognition and navigation.

- **IMUs (Inertial Measurement Units):** Track motion and orientation using accelerometers and gyroscopes.

- **Ultrasonic Sensors:** Detect obstacles by emitting sound waves and measuring their return time.

- **GPS (Global Positioning System):** Provides location data, essential for outdoor navigation.

Benefits of Sensor Integration

- **Enhanced Perception:** Combining data from multiple sensors provides a richer and more accurate representation of the environment.

- **Redundancy:** Multiple sensors can compensate for each other's limitations, increasing system reliability.

- **Improved Accuracy:** Fusion of sensor data can reduce noise and errors, leading to more precise measurements.

- **Versatility:** Enables robots to operate in diverse environments by adapting to different sensor inputs.

Steps to Integrate Sensors in ROS2

Integrating sensors into your ROS2-based robotic system involves several key steps:

1. **Selecting Appropriate Sensors:**

   o Determine the requirements of your application (e.g., indoor vs. outdoor, speed of operation).

   o Choose sensors that provide the necessary data types and ranges.

2. **Connecting Sensors to the Robot:**

   o Physically mount the sensors on the robot.

   o Ensure proper wiring and power supply to each sensor.

3. **Configuring Sensor Drivers:**

   o Install and configure ROS2 drivers for each sensor.

- o Drivers translate raw sensor data into ROS2 messages.

4. **Launching Sensor Nodes:**

- o Use ROS2 launch files to start sensor nodes and ensure they communicate effectively within the ROS2 ecosystem.

5. **Synchronizing Sensor Data:**

- o Implement synchronization mechanisms to align data streams from different sensors, ensuring temporal consistency.

6. **Validating Sensor Integration:**

- o Test each sensor individually and in combination to verify accurate data acquisition and processing.

Diagram 1: Sensor Integration Architecture

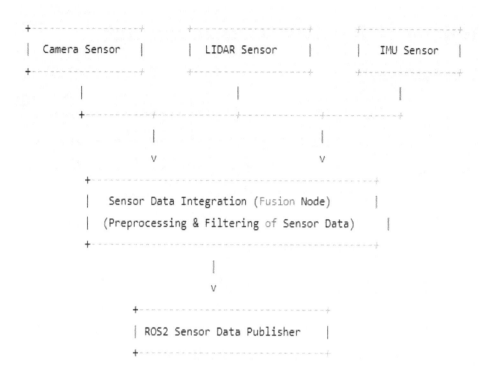

Description: This diagram illustrates the architecture of a ROS2-based sensor integration system. It showcases how different sensors like **LIDAR**, cameras, and **IMU**s connect to the robot, how sensor data is published to **ROS2** topics, and how perception nodes subscribe to these topics to process the data.

Perception and Computer Vision

Implementing Object Detection and Recognition

Imagine a robot that can not only move around but also **recognize objects, interpret gestures**, and **navigate complex environments** seamlessly. Achieving this level of intelligence requires robust **Perception** and **Computer Vision** systems. Let's delve into how to implement object detection and recognition in your robotic applications.

What is Perception in Robotics?

Perception refers to the ability of a robot to interpret sensory data to understand its environment. It involves processing information from sensors to identify objects, recognize patterns, and make sense of the surroundings. **Computer Vision** is a critical component of perception, enabling robots to analyze and interpret visual data.

Object Detection vs. Object Recognition

- **Object Detection:** Identifies and locates objects within an image or a frame. It provides bounding boxes around detected objects.

- **Object Recognition:** Classifies identified objects into predefined categories based on their features.

Tools and Libraries for Computer Vision in ROS2

- **OpenCV:** An open-source computer vision library that provides a wide range of tools for image processing and analysis.

- **TensorFlow/PyTorch:** Deep learning frameworks used for training and deploying object detection and recognition models.

- **YOLO (You Only Look Once):** A real-time object detection system that is fast and efficient.

- **SSD (Single Shot MultiBox Detector):** Another real-time object detection system known for its speed and accuracy.

Steps to Implement Object Detection and Recognition

1. **Capturing Images:**

   o Use cameras to capture real-time images or video streams.

   o Ensure proper lighting and camera positioning for optimal image quality.

2. **Preprocessing Images:**

   o Resize and normalize images to match the input requirements of the detection model.

   o Apply filters to reduce noise and enhance features.

3. **Running Detection Models:**

   o Utilize pre-trained models like YOLO or SSD for object detection.

   o Implement custom models using TensorFlow or PyTorch for specialized tasks.

4. **Post-processing Detection Results:**

   o Apply Non-Maximum Suppression (NMS) to eliminate overlapping bounding boxes.

   o Filter detections based on confidence scores to reduce false positives.

5. **Integrating with ROS2:**

   o Create ROS2 nodes that handle image acquisition, processing, and publishing detection results.

   o Subscribe to detection results for further actions like navigation or interaction.

6. **Visualizing Results:**

   o Use tools like RViz2 or custom visualization scripts to display detection bounding boxes and labels on images.

Example: Implementing YOLO Object Detection in ROS2

Let's walk through a basic implementation of YOLO-based object detection within a ROS2 node.

1. **Prerequisites:**

   - **YOLO Model Files:** Download the YOLO configuration and weights files.

   - **OpenCV Installation:**

bash

```bash
pip install opencv-python
```

2. **Create yolo_object_detection_node.py:**

python

```python
import rclpy
from rclpy.node import Node
from sensor_msgs.msg import Image
from cv_bridge import CvBridge
import cv2
import numpy as np

class YOLOObjectDetectionNode(Node):
    def __init__(self):

        super().__init__('yolo_object_detection_node')
```

```python
        self.subscription =
self.create_subscription(
            Image,
            'camera/image',
            self.listener_callback,
            10)
        self.subscription  # prevent unused
variable warning
        self.bridge = CvBridge()

        # Load YOLO
        self.net =
cv2.dnn.readNet('yolov3.weights', 'yolov3.cfg')
        self.layer_names =
self.net.getLayerNames()
        self.output_layers = [self.layer_names[i
- 1] for i in self.net.getUnconnectedOutLayers()]
        self.classes = []
        with open('coco.names', 'r') as f:
            self.classes = [line.strip() for line
in f.readlines()]
        self.colors = np.random.uniform(0, 255,
size=(len(self.classes), 3))
        self.get_logger().info('YOLO Object
Detection Node has been started.')

    def listener_callback(self, msg):
```

```
        # Convert ROS Image message to OpenCV
image
        cv_image = self.bridge.imgmsg_to_cv2(msg,
desired_encoding='bgr8')
        height, width, channels = cv_image.shape

        # Detecting objects
        blob = cv2.dnn.blobFromImage(cv_image,
0.00392, (416, 416), (0, 0, 0), True, crop=False)
        self.net.setInput(blob)
        outs =
self.net.forward(self.output_layers)

        # Initialization
        class_ids = []
        confidences = []
        boxes = []

        # For each detection from each output
layer
        for out in outs:
            for detection in out:
                scores = detection[5:]
                class_id = np.argmax(scores)
                confidence = scores[class_id]
                if confidence > 0.5:
                    # Object detected
```

```
            center_x = int(detection[0] *
width)
            center_y = int(detection[1] *
height)
        w = int(detection[2] * width)
        h = int(detection[3] *
height)


        # Rectangle coordinates
        x = int(center_x - w / 2)
        y = int(center_y - h / 2)


        boxes.append([x, y, w, h])

confidences.append(float(confidence))
            class_ids.append(class_id)

    # Applying Non-Maximum Suppression
    indexes = cv2.dnn.NMSBoxes(boxes,
confidences, 0.5, 0.4)

    # Draw bounding boxes
    font = cv2.FONT_HERSHEY_PLAIN
    for i in range(len(boxes)):
        if i in indexes:
            x, y, w, h = boxes[i]
            label =
str(self.classes[class_ids[i]])
```

```python
            confidence = confidences[i]
            color = self.colors[class_ids[i]]
            cv2.rectangle(cv_image, (x, y),
(x + w, y + h), color, 2)
            cv2.putText(cv_image, f"{label}
{confidence:.2f}", (x, y + 30), font, 3, color,
3)


        # Publish or display the image as needed
        # For demonstration, we'll display it
using OpenCV
        cv2.imshow("YOLO Object Detection",
cv_image)
        cv2.waitKey(1)


def main(args=None):
    rclpy.init(args=args)
    node = YOLOObjectDetectionNode()
    try:
        rclpy.spin(node)
    except KeyboardInterrupt:
        pass
    node.destroy_node()
    rclpy.shutdown()
    cv2.destroyAllWindows()


if __name__ == '__main__':
    main()
```

- o **Explanation:**
  - **Loading YOLO:** The node loads the YOLO model and configuration files.
  - **Image Callback:** Converts incoming ROS image messages to OpenCV images, processes them through YOLO to detect objects, applies Non-Maximum Suppression to eliminate redundant boxes, and draws bounding boxes with labels.
  - **Visualization:** Displays the processed image with detected objects in real-time using OpenCV's imshow.

3. **Update setup.py:**

Add the YOLO object detection node to console_scripts:

python

```python
entry_points={
    'console_scripts': [
        'hello_node =
hello_world.hello_node:main',
        'publisher_node =
hello_world.publisher_node:main',
        'subscriber_node =
hello_world.subscriber_node:main',
```

```
        'add_two_ints_service =
hello_world.add_two_ints_service:main',
        'add_two_ints_client =
hello_world.add_two_ints_client:main',
        'lifecycle_node =
hello_world.lifecycle_node:main',
        'parameter_node =
hello_world.parameter_node:main',
        'async_sensor_node =
hello_world.async_sensor_node:main',
        'object_recognition_node =
hello_world.object_recognition_node:main',
        'image_classification_node =
hello_world.image_classification_node:main',
        'sensor_clustering_node =
hello_world.sensor_clustering_node:main',
        'yolo_object_detection_node =
hello_world.yolo_object_detection_node:main',
    ],
},
```

4. Make the Script Executable:

```bash
chmod +x yolo_object_detection_node.py
```

5. Build and Source the Workspace:

```bash
```

```
cd ~/ros2_ws
colcon build --packages-select hello_world
source install/setup.bash
```

6. **Run the YOLO Object Detection Node:**

```
bash
```

```
ros2 run hello_world yolo_object_detection_node
```

Expected Output:

A window titled "YOLO Object Detection" will open, displaying the camera feed with bounding boxes and labels around detected objects.

Best Practices for Perception and Computer Vision

- **Optimize Performance:** Use lightweight models or hardware acceleration (e.g., GPUs) to ensure real-time processing.

- **Handle Occlusions:** Implement algorithms that can handle partial visibility of objects.

- **Calibrate Sensors:** Ensure accurate sensor calibration to improve detection and recognition accuracy.

- **Maintain Lighting Conditions:** Consistent lighting enhances the performance of computer vision algorithms.

- **Test in Diverse Environments:** Validate your perception system in various settings to ensure robustness.

Path Planning and Navigation

Algorithms for Autonomous Movement

Have you ever marveled at how a self-driving car smoothly maneuvers through traffic or how a vacuum robot navigates around furniture? The magic behind these seamless movements lies in sophisticated **Path Planning and Navigation** algorithms. These algorithms enable robots to chart efficient and safe paths from one point to another while avoiding obstacles and adapting to dynamic environments.

What is Path Planning?

Path Planning involves computing a trajectory that a robot should follow to move from its current location to a desired destination. It takes into account the robot's kinematics, dynamics, and the environment's geometry to generate feasible paths.

Key Components of Navigation in Robotics

1. Localization:

   o Determining the robot's position within its environment.

- o Techniques include SLAM (Simultaneous Localization and Mapping) and GPS-based localization.

2. **Mapping:**

- o Creating a representation of the robot's environment.
- o Can be grid-based, feature-based, or topological.

3. **Path Planning:**

- o Computing the optimal path from the current position to the goal.
- o Must consider obstacles, terrain, and robot constraints.

4. **Control:**

- o Executing the planned path through motion commands.
- o Ensures the robot follows the trajectory accurately.

Common Path Planning Algorithms

1. **A* (A-Star) Algorithm:**

- o **Type:** Graph-based search algorithm.
- o **Use Case:** Optimal pathfinding on a grid or graph with known cost functions.

- Pros: Guarantees the shortest path if the heuristic is admissible.
- Cons: Can be computationally intensive for large maps.

2. **Dijkstra's Algorithm:**

- **Type:** Graph-based search algorithm.
- **Use Case:** Finding the shortest path without heuristics.
- **Pros:** Guarantees the shortest path.
- **Cons:** Slower compared to A^* due to lack of heuristics.

3. **RRT (Rapidly-exploring Random Tree):**

- **Type:** Sampling-based algorithm.
- **Use Case:** High-dimensional spaces, dynamic environments.
- **Pros:** Efficient for complex spaces, handles dynamic obstacles.
- **Cons:** Does not guarantee the shortest path.

4. **D* (Dynamic A*) Algorithm:**

- **Type:** Incremental search algorithm.
- **Use Case:** Environments with changing obstacles.

- o **Pros:** Reuses previous search efforts, efficient for dynamic environments.

- o **Cons:** More complex to implement than A^*.

5. **Potential Fields:**

- o **Type:** Gradient-based algorithm.

- o **Use Case:** Real-time obstacle avoidance.

- o **Pros:** Simple and fast.

- o **Cons:** Can get stuck in local minima, not suitable for complex environments.

Diagram 2: Path Planning Algorithms Comparison

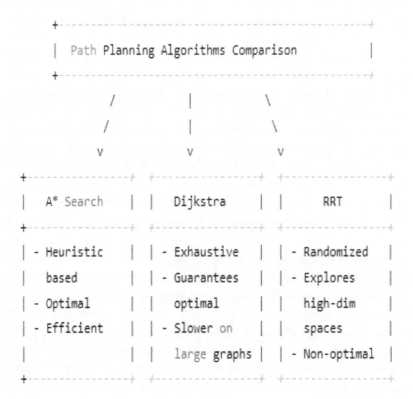

```
+--------------------------------------------------+
|  Path Planning Algorithms Comparison             |
+--------------------------------------------------+

        /            |            \
       /             |             \
      v              v              v
+----------------+ +----------------+ +----------------+
|  A* Search     | |  Dijkstra      | |     RRT        |
+----------------+ +----------------+ +----------------+
| - Heuristic    | | - Exhaustive   | | - Randomized   |
|   based        | | - Guarantees   | | - Explores     |
| - Optimal      | |   optimal      | |   high-dim     |
| - Efficient    | | - Slower on    | |   spaces       |
|                | |   large graphs | | - Non-optimal  |
+----------------+ +----------------+ +----------------+
```

Description: This diagram compares various path planning algorithms based on their characteristics such as search type, optimality, computational complexity, and suitability for different environments. It provides a clear overview to help in selecting the appropriate algorithm for specific robotic applications.

Implementing Path Planning in ROS2

Implementing path planning algorithms in ROS2 involves integrating perception, localization, and control modules to enable autonomous navigation. Let's explore how to set up a basic path planning system using the A^* algorithm.

Steps to Implement A^* Path Planning

1. **Prerequisites:**

    - **ROS2 Installation:** Ensure ROS2 is installed and configured.

    - **Map of the Environment:** Create or obtain a map (e.g., occupancy grid) of the robot's operating area.

    - **Localization Setup:** Implement a localization system to track the robot's position on the map.

2. **Creating the Path Planning Node:**

```python

import rclpy
```

```python
from rclpy.node import Node
from nav_msgs.msg import OccupancyGrid, Path
from geometry_msgs.msg import PoseStamped
import heapq


class AStarPlanner(Node):
    def __init__(self):
        super().__init__('a_star_planner')
        self.subscription = self.create_subscription(
            OccupancyGrid,
            'map',
            self.map_callback,
            10)
        self.publisher = self.create_publisher(Path, 'planned_path', 10)
        self.current_position = None
        self.goal_position = None
        self.map_data = None
        self.width = 0
        self.height = 0
        self.resolution = 0.0
        self.origin = None
        self.get_logger().info('AStarPlanner Node has been started.')

    def map_callback(self, msg):
        self.map_data = msg.data
```

```
        self.width = msg.info.width
        self.height = msg.info.height
        self.resolution = msg.info.resolution
        self.origin = msg.info.origin
        self.get_logger().info('Map received.')
        # After receiving the map, set start and
goal positions
        self.set_start_and_goal()


    def set_start_and_goal(self):
        # For demonstration, set start and goal
positions manually
        self.current_position = (10, 10)   #
Example coordinates
        self.goal_position = (50, 50)       #
Example coordinates
        self.get_logger().info(f'Start:
{self.current_position}, Goal:
{self.goal_position}')
        path = self.a_star(self.current_position,
self.goal_position)
        if path:
            self.publish_path(path)
        else:
            self.get_logger().warn('No path
found.')


    def a_star(self, start, goal):
```

```
def heuristic(a, b):
    return abs(a[0] - b[0]) + abs(a[1] - b[1])


open_set = []
heapq.heappush(open_set, (0 + heuristic(start, goal), 0, start, [start]))
closed_set = set()

while open_set:
    _, cost, current, path = heapq.heappop(open_set)
    if current == goal:
        self.get_logger().info(f'Path found: {path}')
        return path
    if current in closed_set:
        continue
    closed_set.add(current)

    neighbors = self.get_neighbors(current)
    for neighbor in neighbors:
        if neighbor in closed_set:
            continue
        new_cost = cost + 1  # Assuming uniform cost
```

```
            heapq.heappush(open_set,
(new_cost + heuristic(neighbor, goal), new_cost,
neighbor, path + [neighbor]))
        return None

    def get_neighbors(self, node):
        x, y = node
        neighbors = [
            (x+1, y),
            (x-1, y),
            (x, y+1),
            (x, y-1)
        ]
        valid_neighbors = []
        for nx, ny in neighbors:
            if 0 <= nx < self.width and 0 <= ny <
self.height:
                index = ny * self.width + nx
                if self.map_data[index] == 0:  #
0 represents free space
                    valid_neighbors.append((nx,
ny))
        return valid_neighbors

    def publish_path(self, path):
        path_msg = Path()
        path_msg.header.frame_id = 'map'
        for point in path:
```

```
        pose = PoseStamped()
        pose.pose.position.x = point[0] *
self.resolution + self.origin.position.x
        pose.pose.position.y = point[1] *
self.resolution + self.origin.position.y
        pose.pose.position.z = 0.0
        path_msg.poses.append(pose)
    self.publisher.publish(path_msg)
    self.get_logger().info('Planned path
published.')


def main(args=None):
    rclpy.init(args=args)
    planner = AStarPlanner()
    try:
        rclpy.spin(planner)
    except KeyboardInterrupt:
        pass
    planner.destroy_node()
    rclpy.shutdown()


if __name__ == '__main__':
    main()
```

- Explanation:

  - **Map Callback:** Receives the occupancy grid map and initiates the path planning process.

- **A* Implementation:** Uses a simple A* algorithm to find the shortest path from the start to the goal position.

- **Path Publishing:** Publishes the planned path as a ROS2 Path message for other nodes (e.g., control) to consume.

3. **Update setup.py:**

Add the A* planner node to console_scripts:

python

```python
entry_points={
    'console_scripts': [
        'hello_node =
hello_world.hello_node:main',
        'publisher_node =
hello_world.publisher_node:main',
        'subscriber_node =
hello_world.subscriber_node:main',
        'add_two_ints_service =
hello_world.add_two_ints_service:main',
        'add_two_ints_client =
hello_world.add_two_ints_client:main',
        'lifecycle_node =
hello_world.lifecycle_node:main',
        'parameter_node =
hello_world.parameter_node:main',
```

```
      'async_sensor_node =
hello_world.async_sensor_node:main',
        'object_recognition_node =
hello_world.object_recognition_node:main',
        'image_classification_node =
hello_world.image_classification_node:main',
        'sensor_clustering_node =
hello_world.sensor_clustering_node:main',
        'yolo_object_detection_node =
hello_world.yolo_object_detection_node:main',
        'a_star_planner_node =
hello_world.a_star_planner_node:main',
    ],
},
```

4. Make the Script Executable:

```bash

chmod +x a_star_planner_node.py
```

5. Build and Source the Workspace:

```bash

cd ~/ros2_ws
colcon build --packages-select hello_world
source install/setup.bash
```

6. Run the A* Planner Node:

```bash

```

```
ros2 run hello_world a_star_planner_node
```

Expected Output:

```
less
```

```
[INFO] [a_star_planner_node]: AStarPlanner Node
has been started.
[INFO] [a_star_planner_node]: Map received.
[INFO] [a_star_planner_node]: Start: (10, 10),
Goal: (50, 50)
[INFO] [a_star_planner_node]: Path found: [(10,
10), (11, 10), ..., (50, 50)]
[INFO] [a_star_planner_node]: Planned path
published.
```

Best Practices for Path Planning and Navigation

- **Dynamic Re-planning:** Implement mechanisms to update the path in real-time if new obstacles are detected.

- **Obstacle Avoidance:** Integrate sensor data to dynamically avoid unforeseen obstacles.

- **Energy Efficiency:** Optimize paths to minimize energy consumption, extending the robot's operational time.

- **Safety Margins:** Incorporate safety buffers around obstacles to prevent collisions.

- **Multi-robot Coordination:** If deploying multiple robots, ensure path planning accounts for inter-robot interactions to avoid conflicts.

Hands-On Project: Building a Smart Mobile Robot

Overview

Now that you've mastered sensor integration, perception, and path planning, it's time to apply your knowledge by building a **Smart Mobile Robot**. This hands-on project will guide you through integrating sensors, implementing object detection, planning autonomous paths, and bringing it all together to create a robot that can navigate its environment intelligently.

Project Objectives

- **Integrate Multiple Sensors:** Combine data from LIDAR and cameras to perceive the environment.

- **Implement Object Detection:** Use computer vision to identify and classify objects.

- **Plan Autonomous Paths:** Navigate from start to goal while avoiding obstacles.

- **Execute Motion Commands:** Control the robot's movement based on planned paths.

- **Ensure Real-Time Operation:** Maintain responsiveness through asynchronous programming.

Components Required

1. **Robot Platform:**

   - Differential drive mobile robot (e.g., TurtleBot3)

2. **Sensors:**

   - **LIDAR:** For obstacle detection and mapping.

   - **RGB Camera:** For object detection and recognition.

   - **IMU:** For orientation and motion tracking.

3. **Computing Unit:**

   - Onboard computer (e.g., Raspberry Pi, NVIDIA Jetson)

4. **Power Supply:**

   - Batteries compatible with the robot platform and sensors.

5. **ROS2 Software Stack:**

   - Pre-installed on the computing unit.

Step-by-Step Guide

Step 1: Setting Up the Hardware

1. **Assemble the Robot Platform:**

   - Follow the manufacturer's instructions to assemble the mobile robot.

- ○ Ensure all components are securely mounted.

2. **Install Sensors:**

- ○ Mount the **LIDAR** on top of the robot to provide a 360-degree view.

- ○ Attach the **RGB** camera facing forward for object detection.

- ○ Connect the **IMU** to accurately track the robot's orientation.

3. **Connect the Computing Unit:**

- ○ Secure the onboard computer to the robot chassis.

- ○ Ensure all sensors are properly connected to the computing unit via appropriate interfaces (**USB**, **UART**, etc.).

4. **Power Up the System:**

- ○ Connect the power supply, ensuring all components receive the necessary voltage and current.

Step 2: Configuring ROS2 for Sensor Integration

1. **Launch Sensor Drivers:**

   - ○ **LIDAR Driver:**

```bash
ros2 run rplidar_ros rplidar_composition
```

- ○ **Camera Driver:**

bash

```
ros2 run usb_cam usb_cam_node_exe
```
- ○ **IMU Driver:**

bash

```
ros2 run imu_filter_madgwick imu_filter_node
```

2. **Verify Sensor Data Streams:**

- ○ Use ROS2 topics to confirm data is being published.

bash

```
ros2 topic list
ros2 topic echo /scan
ros2 topic echo /camera/image_raw
ros2 topic echo /imu/data
```

Step 3: Implementing Object Detection

1. **Run the YOLO Object Detection Node:**

bash

```
ros2 run hello_world yolo_object_detection_node
```

- ○ **Functionality:** Detects and recognizes objects in the camera feed, displaying bounding boxes and labels in real-time.

2. **Visualize Detection Results:**

   o Ensure the object detection window displays detected objects accurately.

   o Adjust camera settings if detections are unclear.

Step 4: Mapping and Localization

1. **Run SLAM for Mapping:**

bash

```
ros2 launch slam_toolbox online_async_launch.py
```

   o **Functionality:** Creates a real-time occupancy grid map of the environment using LIDAR data.

2. **Visualize the Map in RViz2:**

bash

```
ros2 run rviz2 rviz2
```

   o **Add Map Display:** Configure RViz2 to display the occupancy grid map.

Step 5: Path Planning and Navigation

1. **Run the A* Path Planner Node:**

bash

```
ros2 run hello_world a_star_planner_node
```

   o **Functionality:** Computes an optimal path from the robot's current position to a predefined goal.

2. **Visualize the Planned Path:**

   o In RViz2, add the Path display to visualize the computed trajectory.

3. **Implement Movement Control:**

```python
import rclpy
from rclpy.node import Node
from nav_msgs.msg import Path
from geometry_msgs.msg import Twist

class MovementController(Node):
    def __init__(self):
        super().__init__('movement_controller')
        self.subscription = self.create_subscription(
            Path,
            'planned_path',
            self.path_callback,
            10)
        self.publisher = self.create_publisher(Twist, 'cmd_vel', 10)

        self.get_logger().info('MovementController Node has been started.')

    def path_callback(self, msg):
```

```
    if not msg.poses:
        return
    # Simple controller: Move towards the
first point in the path
    target_pose = msg.poses[0].pose
    twist = Twist()
    twist.linear.x = 0.5  # Move forward at
0.5 m/s
    twist.angular.z = 0.0
    self.publisher.publish(twist)
    self.get_logger().info(f'Moving towards:
({target_pose.position.x},
{target_pose.position.y})')


def main(args=None):
    rclpy.init(args=args)
    controller = MovementController()
    try:
        rclpy.spin(controller)
    except KeyboardInterrupt:
        pass
    controller.destroy_node()
    rclpy.shutdown()


if __name__ == '__main__':
    main()
```

- **Explanation:**

- **MovementController Node:** Subscribes to the planned_path topic and publishes velocity commands to cmd_vel to drive the robot towards the first waypoint in the path.

- **Simple Control Logic:** Moves the robot forward at a constant speed towards the target.

4. **Update setup.py:**

Add the movement controller node to console_scripts:

python

```
entry_points={
    'console_scripts': [
        'hello_node =
hello_world.hello_node:main',
        'publisher_node =
hello_world.publisher_node:main',
        'subscriber_node =
hello_world.subscriber_node:main',
        'add_two_ints_service =
hello_world.add_two_ints_service:main',
        'add_two_ints_client =
hello_world.add_two_ints_client:main',
        'lifecycle_node =
hello_world.lifecycle_node:main',
```

```
        'parameter_node =
hello_world.parameter_node:main',
        'async_sensor_node =
hello_world.async_sensor_node:main',
        'object_recognition_node =
hello_world.object_recognition_node:main',
        'image_classification_node =
hello_world.image_classification_node:main',
        'sensor_clustering_node =
hello_world.sensor_clustering_node:main',
        'yolo_object_detection_node =
hello_world.yolo_object_detection_node:main',
        'a_star_planner_node =
hello_world.a_star_planner_node:main',
        'movement_controller_node =
hello_world.movement_controller_node:main',
    ],
},
```

5. Make the Script Executable:

```bash
chmod +x movement_controller_node.py
```

6. Build and Source the Workspace:

```bash
cd ~/ros2_ws
colcon build --packages-select hello_world
```

```
source install/setup.bash
```

7. **Run the Movement Controller Node:**

```bash

```

```
ros2 run hello_world movement_controller_node
```

Expected Outcome:

The robot begins to move towards the predefined goal, following the planned path while avoiding obstacles.

Best Practices for Path Planning and Navigation

- **Dynamic Re-planning:** Implement re-planning mechanisms to adapt to changing environments or unexpected obstacles.

- **Obstacle Avoidance:** Continuously monitor sensor data to detect and avoid new obstacles along the path.

- **Energy Efficiency:** Optimize movement commands to conserve energy, especially for battery-powered robots.

- **Robust Localization:** Ensure accurate localization to maintain reliability in navigation.

- **Safety Protocols:** Implement emergency stop mechanisms to handle critical failures or unsafe conditions.

Summary

In **Chapter 6: Building Intelligent Systems**, we've embarked on an exciting journey to integrate sensors, implement perception algorithms, and develop autonomous navigation capabilities in your robotic systems. Here's a quick recap of what we've covered:

1. **Sensor Integration:**

   o **Working with LIDAR, Cameras, and Other Sensors:** Explored the importance of integrating multiple sensors to enhance perception and reliability.

   o **Sensor Integration Architecture:** Illustrated how various sensors connect to ROS2 topics and how perception nodes process the data.

2. **Perception and Computer Vision:**

   o **Implementing Object Detection and Recognition:** Learned how to utilize computer vision techniques and models like YOLO for real-time object detection.

   o **Object Detection Pipeline:** Detailed the steps from image acquisition to visualization of detected objects.

3. **Path Planning and Navigation:**

   o **Algorithms for Autonomous Movement:** Reviewed key path planning algorithms including A*, Dijkstra's, RRT, D*, and Potential Fields.

- ○ **Path Planning Algorithms Comparison:** Compared various algorithms based on their strengths and suitability for different environments.

4. **Hands-On Project: Building a Smart Mobile Robot:**

- ○ **Sensor Integration, Object Detection, Path Planning, and Movement Control:** Applied the concepts by integrating sensors, implementing object detection, planning paths, and controlling robot movement.

5. **Visual Diagrams:**

- ○ Provided comprehensive diagrams to visualize sensor integration, object detection pipelines, path planning algorithm comparisons, and ML integration workflows, reinforcing the practical application of the discussed concepts.

Final Encouragement

Building intelligent systems is a blend of creativity, technical prowess, and relentless experimentation. As you integrate sensors, refine perception algorithms, and perfect path planning, remember that each challenge is an opportunity to innovate and enhance your robotic creations. Embrace the complexities, stay curious, and continue pushing the boundaries of what's possible. Your journey towards creating

truly autonomous and intelligent robots is well underway—
keep moving forward!

Chapter 7: Machine Learning in Robotics

Welcome to **Chapter 7: Machine Learning in Robotics**! As robots transition from being mere programmed machines to intelligent autonomous agents, **Machine Learning (ML)** plays a pivotal role in this transformation. ML empowers robots to learn from data, adapt to new environments, and perform complex tasks with minimal human intervention. In this chapter, we'll explore the fundamentals of machine learning, delve into its various types, examine its applications in robotics, and engage in a hands-on project to train a robot for autonomous navigation. Let's embark on this journey to infuse intelligence into your robotic creations!

Introduction to Machine Learning

What is Machine Learning?

Have you ever wondered how your smartphone predicts the next word you're going to type or how self-driving cars recognize pedestrians? The magic behind these capabilities is **Machine Learning (ML)**. At its core, ML is a subset of artificial intelligence that enables systems to learn and improve from experience without being explicitly programmed. Instead of following rigid instructions, ML algorithms analyze data, identify patterns, and make decisions based on that analysis.

Why Machine Learning Matters in Robotics

Imagine trying to navigate a robot through a cluttered room using only pre-programmed instructions. Every new obstacle would require manual updates to the robot's code, making the system inflexible and time-consuming to maintain. **Machine Learning** revolutionizes this scenario by allowing robots to:

- **Adapt to Dynamic Environments:** Learn from changing conditions and adjust their actions accordingly.

- **Enhance Perception:** Improve object detection, recognition, and interpretation using vast amounts of sensory data.

- **Optimize Performance:** Continuously refine movements and strategies for efficiency and effectiveness.

- **Enable Autonomy:** Make informed decisions without constant human oversight.

In essence, ML transforms robots from static machines into intelligent agents capable of interacting seamlessly with their surroundings.

Supervised, Unsupervised, and Reinforcement Learning

Machine Learning encompasses various approaches, each suited to different types of problems and data. Understanding these types is crucial for selecting the right technique for your robotic applications.

Supervised Learning

Supervised Learning is akin to learning with a teacher. The algorithm is trained on a labeled dataset, meaning each input data point is paired with the correct output. The goal is for the model to learn the mapping from inputs to outputs so it can make accurate predictions on unseen data.

Example in Robotics:

- **Object Recognition:** Training a robot to identify different objects by providing labeled images (e.g., "apple," "banana," "cup").

How It Works:

1. **Data Collection:** Gather a large dataset of inputs (e.g., images) and their corresponding labels.

2. **Model Training:** Use algorithms like Support Vector Machines (SVM), Decision Trees, or Neural Networks to learn from the data.

3. **Prediction:** Apply the trained model to new, unlabeled data to predict the output.

Pros:

- High accuracy with sufficient labeled data.

- Clear evaluation metrics.

Cons:

- Requires extensive labeled datasets.

- May not generalize well to data outside the training distribution.

Unsupervised Learning

Unsupervised Learning is like exploring without a map. The algorithm is provided with unlabeled data and must find inherent structures, patterns, or relationships within the data on its own.

Example in Robotics:

- **Clustering Sensor Data:** Grouping similar sensor readings to identify different operational modes or environmental conditions.

How It Works:

1. **Data Collection:** Gather a dataset without labels.

2. **Model Training:** Use algorithms like K-Means Clustering, Principal Component Analysis (PCA), or Hierarchical Clustering to uncover patterns.

3. **Analysis:** Interpret the discovered structures to inform robotic behavior.

Pros:

- No need for labeled data.

- Can discover hidden patterns in data.

Cons:

- More challenging to evaluate model performance.

- May find patterns that are not meaningful for the task.

Reinforcement Learning

Reinforcement Learning (RL) is like training a dog with rewards and punishments. An agent learns to make decisions by performing actions in an environment to maximize cumulative rewards.

Example in Robotics:

- **Autonomous Navigation:** Teaching a robot to navigate a maze by rewarding it for reaching the exit and penalizing it for hitting walls.

How It Works:

1. **Environment Interaction:** The robot interacts with its environment by taking actions.

2. **Reward System:** The environment provides feedback in the form of rewards or penalties based on the robot's actions.

3. **Policy Optimization:** The robot updates its strategy (policy) to maximize the expected rewards over time.

Pros:

- Suitable for sequential decision-making tasks.

- Can handle complex, dynamic environments.

Cons:

- Requires significant computational resources.

- Can be sample inefficient, needing many interactions to learn effectively.

Diagram 1: Types of Machine Learning

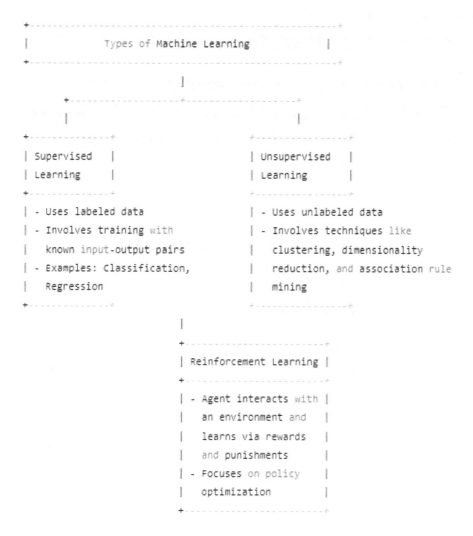

Description: This diagram categorizes Machine Learning into its primary types: Supervised, Unsupervised, and Reinforcement Learning. It illustrates the flow of data and learning processes unique to each type, highlighting their distinct applications and methodologies.

Applying ML to Robotics

Use Cases and Best Practices

Machine Learning offers a plethora of applications in robotics, enhancing capabilities across various domains. Let's explore some prominent use cases and best practices to ensure successful ML integration.

Use Cases in Robotics

1. Object Detection and Recognition:

   o **Description:** Identifying and classifying objects within the robot's environment.

   o **Applications:** Warehouse robots locating items, service robots recognizing household objects.

2. Autonomous Navigation:

   o **Description:** Enabling robots to navigate from point A to B without human intervention.

   o **Applications:** Self-driving cars, drones navigating through obstacles.

3. Manipulation and Grasping:

   o **Description:** Allowing robots to handle and manipulate objects with precision.

   o **Applications:** Industrial robots assembling products, assistive robots aiding in daily tasks.

4. **Human-Robot Interaction:**

   o **Description:** Facilitating seamless interaction between humans and robots.

   o **Applications:** Social robots engaging with users, collaborative robots working alongside humans.

5. **Predictive Maintenance:**

   o **Description:** Anticipating and preventing system failures through data analysis.

   o **Applications:** Manufacturing robots monitoring their health, autonomous vehicles detecting wear and tear.

Best Practices for ML Integration in Robotics

1. **Define Clear Objectives:**

   o **Why:** Ensures the ML model addresses specific robotic needs.

   o **How:** Outline the problem you aim to solve and the desired outcomes.

2. **Gather Quality Data:**

   o **Why:** ML models rely on data quality for accurate learning.

   o **How:** Collect diverse, representative, and labeled datasets.

3. **Choose the Right Algorithm:**

- o **Why:** Different tasks require different ML approaches.

- o **How:** Assess the problem's nature and select suitable supervised, unsupervised, or reinforcement learning algorithms.

4. **Ensure Computational Efficiency:**

   - o **Why:** Robots often operate in real-time environments with limited resources.

   - o **How:** Optimize models for speed and deploy them on efficient hardware (e.g., NVIDIA Jetson for edge computing).

5. **Implement Robust Testing:**

   - o **Why:** Validates model performance and reliability.

   - o **How:** Use cross-validation, test in diverse scenarios, and perform real-world trials.

6. **Maintain Model Interpretability:**

   - o **Why:** Understanding model decisions aids in debugging and trust.

   - o **How:** Utilize interpretable models or tools that explain complex model behaviors.

7. **Continuous Learning and Adaptation:**

   - o **Why:** Environments change, and models need to adapt.

- o **How:** Implement mechanisms for incremental learning and model updates.

Diagram 2: ML Application in Robotics

```
+- - - - - - - - - - - - - - - - - - - - - - - -+
|           Sensor Data             |
|    (Camera, LIDAR, IMU, etc.)     |
+- - - - - - - - - - - +- - - - - - - - - - - - -+
                |
                v
+- - - - - - - - - - - - - - - - - - - - - - - -+
|   ML-based Perception Module      |
|   (Object Detection, Sensor       |
|        Fusion, etc.)              |
+- - - - - - - - - - - - +- - - - - - - - - - - - -+
                |
                v
+- - - - - - - - - - - - - - - - - - - - - - - -+
|  ML-driven Decision-Making        |
|     (Reinforcement Learning,      |
|    Behavior Trees, etc.)          |
+- - - - - - - - - - - - +- - - - - - - - - - - - -+
                |
                v
+- - - - - - - - - - - - - - - - - - - - - - - -+
|   Robotic Control & Actuation     |
|   (Motor Commands, Trajectory     |
|    Planning, Real-Time Control)   |
+- - - - - - - - - - - - - - - - - - - - - - - -+
```

Description: This diagram showcases the integration of Machine Learning into robotic systems. It illustrates various application areas such as perception, decision-making, and control, highlighting how ML models interact with sensor data and robotic actuators to enable intelligent behaviors.

Deep Learning for Autonomous Systems

Neural Networks and Their Applications

In the realm of Machine Learning, **Deep Learning** stands out as a powerful subset that mimics the human brain's architecture to process complex data. **Neural Networks**, the backbone of Deep Learning, enable robots to perform tasks that require understanding intricate patterns and making nuanced decisions.

What are Neural Networks?

Neural Networks are computational models inspired by the human brain's network of neurons. They consist of layers of interconnected nodes (neurons) that process data through weighted connections. Each neuron applies an activation function to its input to produce an output, allowing the network to learn and model complex relationships within the data.

Key Components of Neural Networks

1. **Input Layer:**

   o **Function:** Receives raw data (e.g., images, sensor readings).

   o **Example:** Pixel values from a camera image.

2. **Hidden Layers:**

   o **Function:** Perform intermediate computations, extracting features and patterns.

   o **Example:** Convolutional layers in image processing.

3. **Output Layer:**

   o **Function:** Produces the final prediction or decision.

   o **Example:** Classification labels (e.g., "apple," "banana") or regression outputs (e.g., steering angle).

4. **Activation Functions:**

   o **Function:** Introduce non-linearity, enabling the network to model complex patterns.

   o **Examples:** ReLU, Sigmoid, Tanh.

5. **Weights and Biases:**

   o **Function:** Parameters that the network learns during training to adjust the influence of inputs.

- o **Example:** Adjusting the strength of connections between neurons based on data.

Types of Neural Networks and Their Applications in Robotics

1. **Convolutional Neural Networks (CNNs):**

   - o **Use Case:** Image and video processing.

   - o **Application:** Object detection, visual recognition, scene understanding.

2. **Recurrent Neural Networks (RNNs):**

   - o **Use Case:** Sequential data processing.

   - o **Application:** Time-series prediction, speech recognition, gesture recognition.

3. **Deep Reinforcement Learning (DRL):**

   - o **Use Case:** Decision-making and control.

   - o **Application:** Autonomous navigation, robotic arm manipulation, game playing.

4. **Generative Adversarial Networks (GANs):**

   - o **Use Case:** Data generation and augmentation.

   - o **Application:** Creating synthetic training data, enhancing image resolution.

5. **Autoencoders:**

- o **Use Case:** Dimensionality reduction and feature learning.

- o **Application:** Anomaly detection, sensor data compression.

How Deep Learning Enhances Autonomous Systems

- **Improved Perception:** Deep Learning models excel at interpreting raw sensory data, enabling robots to understand their environment with high accuracy.

- **Adaptive Behavior:** Models like DRL allow robots to learn optimal actions through interaction, adapting to new challenges autonomously.

- **Enhanced Decision-Making:** Neural networks can process vast amounts of data quickly, facilitating real-time decision-making essential for autonomous operations.

- **Scalability:** Deep Learning models can scale to handle more complex tasks as computational resources increase, ensuring robots remain capable as their environments grow in complexity.

Hands-On Project: Training a Robot to Navigate Using ML

Project Overview

Now that we've covered the theoretical aspects of Machine Learning in robotics, it's time to apply this knowledge through a hands-on project. **Training a Robot to Navigate Using ML** will guide you through the process of enabling a robot to autonomously navigate its environment using Deep Learning techniques.

Project Objectives

- **Implement Autonomous Navigation:** Enable the robot to move from a start point to a destination without human intervention.

- **Obstacle Detection and Avoidance:** Utilize ML models to detect and navigate around obstacles.

- **Path Optimization:** Learn to choose the most efficient path based on environmental data.

- **Real-Time Decision Making:** Ensure the robot can make swift decisions based on sensory inputs.

Components Required

1. **Robot Platform:**

   o Differential drive mobile robot (e.g., TurtleBot3)

2. **Sensors:**

   - o **LIDAR:** For mapping and obstacle detection.

   - o **RGB Camera:** For visual perception and object recognition.

   - o **IMU:** For orientation and motion tracking.

3. **Computing Unit:**

   - o Onboard computer with GPU capabilities (e.g., NVIDIA Jetson Nano)

4. **Software Tools:**

   - o ROS2

   - o TensorFlow or PyTorch

   - o OpenCV

   - o Relevant ML libraries

Step-by-Step Guide

Step 1: Setting Up the Development Environment

1. **Install ROS2:**

   - o Follow the official ROS2 installation guide for your operating system.

2. **Set Up Python Environment:**

   - o Create a virtual environment to manage dependencies.

bash

```
python3 -m venv ml_robotics_env
source ml_robotics_env/bin/activate
```

3. Install Required Libraries:

```bash
pip install tensorflow opencv-python torch
torchvision scikit-learn
```

Step 2: Data Collection

1. Configure Sensor Nodes:

- Launch ROS2 nodes to start publishing data from LIDAR and the camera.

```bash
ros2 launch turtlebot3_gazebo
turtlebot3_world.launch.py
ros2 run turtlebot3_sensors turtlebot3_lidar_node
ros2 run turtlebot3_sensors
turtlebot3_camera_node
```

2. Record Sensor Data:

- Use ROS2 bag to record sensor streams for training purposes.

```bash
ros2 bag record /scan /camera/image_raw /imu/data
```

3. Data Annotation:

- o Label the recorded data if using supervised learning for tasks like obstacle detection.

Step 3: Preprocessing and Preparing the Data

1. Extract Frames from Recorded Data:

```bash
bash
```

```
ros2 bag play your_bag_file.db3
```

- o Use OpenCV to capture frames from the camera feed.

```python
python
```

```python
import cv2
import rosbag
from sensor_msgs.msg import Image
from cv_bridge import CvBridge

bridge = CvBridge()

with rosbag.Bag('your_bag_file.db3') as bag:
    for topic, msg, t in
bag.read_messages(topics=['/camera/image_raw']):
        cv_image = bridge.imgmsg_to_cv2(msg,
desired_encoding='bgr8')
        cv2.imwrite(f'images/frame_{t}.png',
cv_image)
```

2. Data Cleaning:

- ○ Remove corrupted or irrelevant frames.

- ○ Normalize image sizes and color channels.

3. **Data Augmentation:**

- ○ Enhance the dataset by applying transformations like rotation, scaling, and flipping.

python

```
from tensorflow.keras.preprocessing.image import
ImageDataGenerator

datagen = ImageDataGenerator(
    rotation_range=20,
    width_shift_range=0.2,
    height_shift_range=0.2,
    horizontal_flip=True
)

# Example usage
img = cv2.imread('images/frame_1.png')
img = img.reshape((1,) + img.shape)  # Reshape
for Keras
for batch in datagen.flow(img, batch_size=1,
save_to_dir='augmented', save_prefix='frame',
save_format='png'):
    break  # Save one augmented image
```

Step 4: Model Selection and Training

1. **Choose the Right Model:**

    o For obstacle detection, models like **YOLOv3** or **SSD** are suitable.

    o For path planning, consider **Deep Reinforcement Learning** models.

2. **Implement Object Detection with YOLOv3:**

python

```python
import tensorflow as tf
from tensorflow.keras.models import load_model
import cv2
import numpy as np

# Load pre-trained YOLOv3 model
model = load_model('yolov3.h5')

def preprocess_image(image_path):
    img = cv2.imread(image_path)
    img = cv2.resize(img, (416, 416))
    img = img / 255.0
    img = np.expand_dims(img, axis=0)
    return img

def detect_objects(image_path):
    img = preprocess_image(image_path)
    predictions = model.predict(img)
```

```python
    # Further processing for bounding boxes and
labels
    return predictions


# Example usage
predictions =
detect_objects('images/frame_1.png')
```

3. Train a Reinforcement Learning Agent for Navigation:

python

```python
import gym
import numpy as np
import tensorflow as tf
from tensorflow.keras import layers


env = gym.make('CarRacing-v0')


num_actions = env.action_space.shape[0]


# Build a simple policy network
model = tf.keras.Sequential([
    layers.Dense(24, activation='relu',
input_shape=(env.observation_space.shape[0],)),
    layers.Dense(24, activation='relu'),
    layers.Dense(num_actions,
activation='linear')
])
```

```
optimizer = tf.keras.optimizers.Adam(lr=0.001)
loss_fn = tf.keras.losses.MeanSquaredError()

# Training loop (simplified)
for episode in range(1000):
    state = env.reset()
    done = False
    while not done:
        action = model.predict(state.reshape(1, -1))
        next_state, reward, done, info = env.step(action[0])
        # Compute target and update model
        target = reward + 0.95 * np.amax(model.predict(next_state.reshape(1, -1)))
        target_vec = model.predict(state.reshape(1, -1))[0]
        target_vec[np.argmax(action)] = target
        model.fit(state.reshape(1, -1), target_vec.reshape(-1, num_actions), epochs=1, verbose=0)
        state = next_state
```

4. **Validate the Model:**

   o Test the trained model on a separate validation set.

   o Evaluate performance metrics like precision, recall, and F1-score for object detection.

Step 5: Deploying the Model on the Robot

1. Optimize the Model for Deployment:

- o Convert the model to TensorFlow Lite or use model quantization for faster inference.

bash

```
# Convert to TensorFlow Lite
tflite_convert --output_file=yolov3.tflite --
saved_model_dir=yolov3_saved_model
```

2. Integrate with ROS2:

python

```python
import rclpy
from rclpy.node import Node
from sensor_msgs.msg import Image
from cv_bridge import CvBridge
import cv2
import numpy as np
import tensorflow as tf

class MLNavigationNode(Node):
    def __init__(self):
        super().__init__('ml_navigation_node')
        self.subscription =
self.create_subscription(
            Image,
            '/camera/image_raw',
```

```
            self.image_callback,
            10)
        self.publisher =
self.create_publisher(Twist, '/cmd_vel', 10)
        self.bridge = CvBridge()
        self.model =
tf.lite.Interpreter(model_path='yolov3.tflite')
        self.model.allocate_tensors()
        self.input_details =
self.model.get_input_details()
        self.output_details =
self.model.get_output_details()
        self.get_logger().info('MLNavigationNode
has been started.')


    def image_callback(self, msg):
        cv_image = self.bridge.imgmsg_to_cv2(msg,
desired_encoding='bgr8')
        input_data = cv2.resize(cv_image, (416,
416))
        input_data = input_data / 255.0
        input_data = np.expand_dims(input_data,
axis=0).astype(np.float32)

self.model.set_tensor(self.input_details[0]['inde
x'], input_data)
        self.model.invoke()
```

```
        output_data =
self.model.get_tensor(self.output_details[0]['ind
ex'])
        # Process output_data to determine
movement commands
        twist = Twist()
        twist.linear.x = 0.5  # Example command
        twist.angular.z = 0.0
        self.publisher.publish(twist)
        self.get_logger().info('Published
movement command.')


def main(args=None):
    rclpy.init(args=args)
    node = MLNavigationNode()
    try:
        rclpy.spin(node)
    except KeyboardInterrupt:
        pass
    node.destroy_node()
    rclpy.shutdown()


if __name__ == '__main__':
    main()
```

3. Testing and Iteration:

- o Deploy the node and observe the robot's behavior.

- o Fine-tune the model and parameters based on performance.

- o Implement safety measures to handle unexpected scenarios.

Summary

In **Chapter 7: Machine Learning in Robotics**, we've explored the transformative role of Machine Learning in creating intelligent robotic systems. Here's a quick recap of what we've covered:

1. **Introduction to Machine Learning:**

   - o Defined Machine Learning and its significance in robotics.

   - o Discussed how ML transforms robots into intelligent, adaptive agents.

2. **Supervised, Unsupervised, and Reinforcement Learning:**

   - o Explained the three primary types of ML.

   - o Illustrated their unique methodologies and applications within robotics.

3. **Types of Machine Learning Diagram:**

   - o Visualized the distinctions and flows within Supervised, Unsupervised, and Reinforcement Learning.

4. **Applying ML to Robotics:**

   o Explored various use cases such as object detection, autonomous navigation, and predictive maintenance.

   o Highlighted best practices for successful ML integration.

5. **ML Application in Robotics Diagram:**

   o Showcased how ML models interact with sensor data and robotic actuators to enable intelligent behaviors.

6. **Deep Learning for Autonomous Systems:**

   o Delved into Neural Networks, their architectures, and applications in robotics.

   o Discussed the impact of Deep Learning on perception, decision-making, and control.

7. **Deep Learning Architecture Diagram:**

   o Illustrated a typical neural network flow from input data to actionable outputs.

8. **Hands-On Project: Training a Robot to Navigate Using ML:**

   o Guided you through implementing ML models for autonomous navigation.

   o Covered data collection, preprocessing, model training, deployment, and testing.

Final Encouragement

Mastering Machine Learning is a significant milestone in your robotics journey. By leveraging ML techniques, you've unlocked new dimensions of autonomy and intelligence for your robots. Remember, the key to excellence lies in continuous learning and hands-on experimentation. Keep refining your models, experimenting with new algorithms, and pushing the boundaries of what's possible in robotics. Your dedication and curiosity are the driving forces that will propel your robotic creations to new heights of sophistication and capability.

Happy training!

Chapter 8: Multi-Robot Coordination

Welcome to **Chapter 8: Multi-Robot Coordination**—a deep dive into how multiple robots can work together seamlessly to achieve common goals. In today's complex and dynamic environments, a single robot might not be enough to tackle intricate tasks efficiently. By coordinating a team of robots, we can achieve increased productivity, redundancy, scalability, and flexibility. In this chapter, we'll cover the fundamentals of multi-robot systems, explore communication protocols, delve into cooperative task planning, and walk through a hands-on project that demonstrates how to coordinate a team of robots for a common task.

Throughout this chapter, our focus will be on clarity and practical application. We'll break down each concept into digestible, actionable steps while employing relatable analogies and real-world examples. Additionally, visual aids in the form of diagrams and flowcharts will support your understanding and help you visualize the architecture and processes involved in multi-robot coordination.

Fundamentals of Multi-Robot Systems

Benefits and Challenges

Imagine a busy restaurant kitchen where each chef specializes in a different part of the meal—from appetizers to desserts. The collaborative effort of the entire team leads to a seamless dining experience. Similarly, in robotics, coordinating multiple robots can transform a single, isolated unit into a dynamic, efficient team capable of handling complex tasks.

Benefits

1. **Increased Efficiency and Productivity:**

   ○ **Parallel Processing:** Multiple robots can work simultaneously on different segments of a task, reducing overall execution time.

   ○ **Task Specialization:** Robots can be assigned roles based on their capabilities (e.g., one for mapping, another for manipulation), leading to optimized performance.

2. **Redundancy and Robustness:**

   ○ **Fault Tolerance:** If one robot fails or encounters an obstacle, others can compensate, ensuring mission continuity.

   ○ **Enhanced Reliability:** The failure of a single unit does not halt the entire operation.

3. **Scalability:**

- **Modular Expansion:** Systems can be scaled up by simply adding more robots without redesigning the entire architecture.

- **Adaptability:** Multi-robot systems can easily adapt to varying task complexities and environmental conditions.

4. **Flexibility:**

- **Dynamic Task Allocation:** Tasks can be reallocated in real-time based on the current state of each robot.

- **Collaborative Problem Solving:** Robots can share information and collaborate to overcome challenges that might be insurmountable individually.

Challenges

1. **Communication Overhead:**

- **Data Synchronization:** Ensuring that all robots have a consistent view of the environment can be challenging, especially with limited bandwidth.

- **Latency:** Delays in communication can lead to outdated information, affecting coordination.

2. **Complex Coordination Algorithms:**

- o **Task Allocation:** Efficiently distributing tasks among robots requires sophisticated algorithms.

- o **Collision Avoidance:** Ensuring that robots do not interfere with each other while moving is critical.

3. **Resource Management:**

- o **Energy Consumption:** Coordinating multiple robots often means managing battery life and ensuring optimal power usage.

- o **Computational Load:** Complex coordination and data processing can strain onboard computational resources.

4. **Heterogeneity:**

- o **Diverse Capabilities:** In systems with different types of robots, integrating various hardware and software capabilities can be challenging.

- o **Interoperability:** Ensuring that different robots and their components communicate effectively requires standard protocols and interfaces.

Diagram 1: Multi-Robot System Architecture

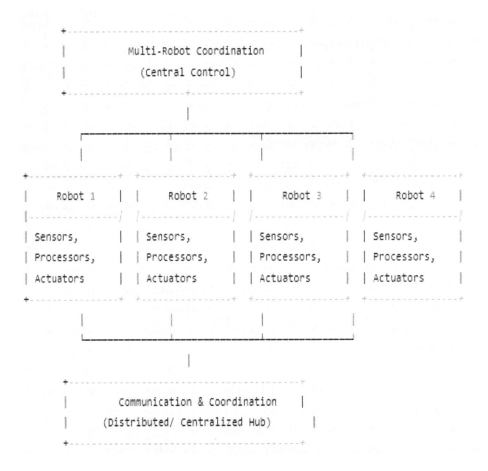

Description:

This diagram presents a simplified vertical architecture of a multi-robot system. It highlights the core components including individual robots (each with its own sensors, processors, and actuators), a central communication hub (or distributed communication framework), and higher-level coordination nodes that manage task allocation and decision-making.

Communication Protocols

Ensuring Seamless Interaction Between Robots

When multiple robots need to work together, effective communication is paramount. The ability to share information reliably and quickly forms the backbone of multi-robot coordination. Let's dive into the communication protocols that facilitate seamless interaction among robots.

Key Communication Concepts

1. **Message Passing:**

   o **Topics:** Robots use topics to publish and subscribe to messages asynchronously, ensuring that data flows between robots without requiring direct connections.

   o **Services:** Provide synchronous communication for request-response interactions, ideal for tasks that require immediate confirmation.

   o **Actions:** Support long-running tasks with continuous feedback, allowing robots to monitor progress and adjust accordingly.

2. **Middleware Solutions:**

   o **DDS (Data Distribution Service):** ROS2 utilizes DDS as its underlying middleware to handle the complex communication needs of distributed systems. DDS ensures real-time performance, reliability, and scalability in data exchange.

- o **Peer-to-Peer Communication:** In some architectures, robots communicate directly with each other without a central coordinator, which can reduce latency and increase robustness.

3. **Networking Protocols:**

- o **TCP/UDP:** Traditional protocols that can be used depending on the reliability and speed requirements.

- o **Custom Protocols:** In some cases, custom communication protocols might be developed to meet the specific needs of the robotic system.

Best Practices for Communication

- **Minimize Latency:** Optimize network configurations and choose the right middleware settings to reduce delays.

- **Ensure Reliability:** Implement error-checking and data validation mechanisms to prevent miscommunication.

- **Scalability:** Use protocols that can handle an increasing number of robots without significant performance degradation.

- **Security:** Encrypt sensitive data and use secure channels to protect communication from unauthorized access.

Diagram 2: Communication Protocols Overview

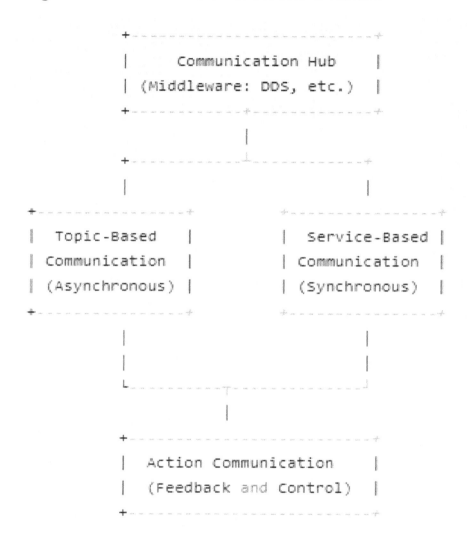

Description:

This diagram provides an overview of the communication protocols used in multi-robot systems. It illustrates how various communication channels—such as topics for asynchronous messaging, services for synchronous interactions, and actions for long-running tasks—enable robust and efficient coordination among robots.

Cooperative Task Planning

Strategies for Efficient Collaboration

Once communication is established, the next step in multi-robot coordination is task planning. Cooperative task planning involves the strategic allocation and scheduling of tasks among multiple robots so that they can work together efficiently. Think of it as choreographing a complex dance where every participant knows their moves and timing.

Key Strategies for Task Planning

1. **Task Allocation:**

    o **Centralized Approach:** A central coordinator assigns tasks to each robot based on their capabilities, current state, and proximity to the task.

    o **Decentralized Approach:** Robots negotiate among themselves to distribute tasks, increasing robustness and scalability.

2. **Scheduling:**

    o **Time-Based Scheduling:** Tasks are scheduled based on specific time slots, ensuring that robots are not idle.

- ○ **Priority-Based Scheduling:** Tasks are prioritized, and robots focus on high-priority tasks first, which is essential in dynamic environments.

3. **Path Coordination:**

   - ○ **Collision Avoidance:** Ensuring that robots do not interfere with each other while performing their tasks.

   - ○ **Optimized Routing:** Selecting routes that minimize travel time and energy consumption while maximizing efficiency.

4. **Dynamic Re-planning:**

   - ○ **Real-Time Adjustments:** As conditions change, robots must be able to adapt their plans on the fly.

   - ○ **Feedback Loops:** Continuous monitoring of task progress and environmental conditions to update plans as needed.

Best Practices for Cooperative Task Planning

- **Define Clear Objectives:** Establish clear goals for each task and how it contributes to the overall mission.

- **Use Efficient Algorithms:** Leverage algorithms such as Auction-Based Task Allocation or Consensus-Based Methods for optimal task distribution.

- **Monitor and Adjust:** Implement systems for real-time monitoring and dynamic re-planning to respond to unexpected changes.

- **Promote Robustness:** Design fault-tolerant systems so that if one robot fails, others can take over its tasks.

Diagram 3: Task Planning Workflow

```
+-------------------------------+
|   Task Definition             |
|   (Objectives, Goals)         |
+-------------------------------+
                |
                ▼
+-------------------------------+
|   Task Allocation             |
|   (Centralized/Decentralized) |
+-------------------------------+
                |
                ▼
+-------------------------------+
|   Scheduling &                |
|   Prioritization              |
+-------------------------------+
                |
                ▼
+-------------------------------+
|   Task Execution              |
|   (Robot Actions)             |
+-------------------------------+
                |
                ▼
+-------------------------------+
|   Feedback &                  |
|   Dynamic Re-planning         |
+-------------------------------+
```

Description:

This diagram outlines the workflow of cooperative task planning in multi-robot systems. It illustrates the process from task definition and allocation to scheduling, execution, and dynamic re-planning. The workflow highlights how feedback from the robots and the environment continuously informs and refines the overall plan.

Hands-On Project: Coordinating a Team of Robots for a Common Task

Project Overview

In this hands-on project, you will learn how to coordinate a team of robots to perform a common task. Imagine a scenario where a fleet of warehouse robots is required to transport items from storage to shipping areas efficiently. This project will guide you through:

- **Establishing Communication:** Setting up a communication framework between multiple robots.

- **Task Allocation:** Distributing tasks among robots based on their capabilities and current locations.

- **Cooperative Task Execution:** Ensuring robots work together seamlessly to avoid collisions and optimize routes.

- **Dynamic Re-planning:** Adjusting the plan in real-time based on environmental changes and task progress.

Project Objectives

- **Efficient Collaboration:** Achieve a coordinated workflow that maximizes productivity.

- **Robust Communication:** Ensure seamless data exchange between all robots.

- **Adaptive Task Planning:** Enable dynamic re-planning in response to unexpected events.

- **Real-Time Control:** Maintain precise control over each robot's actions during task execution.

Components Required

1. **Robotic Platforms:**

   - A team of identical or heterogeneous robots (e.g., TurtleBot3 units or simulated robots in Gazebo).

2. **Sensors:**

   - LIDAR and cameras for mapping and obstacle detection.

   - Optional: Additional sensors such as ultrasonic sensors for enhanced perception.

3. **Communication Infrastructure:**

   - A network (wired or wireless) that supports low-latency communication.

   - ROS2-based middleware for message passing and coordination.

4. **Control System:**

   - A centralized or decentralized controller for task allocation and monitoring.

   - Algorithms for cooperative task planning and dynamic re-planning.

Step-by-Step Guide

Step 1: Establishing the Communication Framework

1. **Set Up ROS2 Network:**

   - Ensure that all robots are connected to the same ROS2 network.

   - Configure ROS2 to use the appropriate middleware (e.g., DDS) for real-time communication.

   - Verify communication by listing ROS2 nodes across robots:

bash

Copy

ros2 node list

2. **Implement a Central Coordination Node:**

   - Create a ROS2 node that acts as a coordinator, responsible for task allocation and monitoring.

- o This node should subscribe to status updates from each robot and publish global task assignments.

Step 2: Task Allocation and Scheduling

1. **Define the Task:**

   - o Clearly specify the common task. For example, "Transport items from storage to shipping."

   - o Define task parameters such as pickup locations, drop-off points, and time constraints.

2. **Develop Task Allocation Algorithm:**

   - o Use a centralized approach where the coordinator assigns tasks based on real-time data.

   - o Alternatively, implement a decentralized algorithm where robots negotiate tasks among themselves.

   - o Implement a simple auction-based mechanism:
     - ▪ Each robot calculates a "cost" based on its distance from the task.
     - ▪ The robot with the lowest cost wins the task.
     - ▪ Publish the winning bid and assign the task.

3. **Schedule Tasks:**

- ○ Prioritize tasks based on urgency and importance.

- ○ Use time-based scheduling to ensure that tasks are executed within specified time windows.

Step 3: Cooperative Task Execution

1. Plan Paths for Each Robot:

- ○ Use path planning algorithms (e.g., A* or RRT) to compute optimal routes for each robot.

- ○ Ensure paths account for dynamic obstacles and potential inter-robot collisions.

- ○ Publish planned paths to each robot via ROS2 topics.

2. Implement Collision Avoidance:

- ○ Integrate real-time sensor data to detect obstacles and adjust paths dynamically.

- ○ Use decentralized communication for local collision avoidance among nearby robots.

3. Monitor and Adjust:

- ○ Continuously monitor the progress of each robot through status messages.

- ○ Implement feedback loops in the coordination node to reassign tasks or re-plan paths if a robot deviates or encounters an unexpected obstacle.

Step 4: Dynamic Re-planning and Adaptation

1. Real-Time Feedback:

- o Ensure each robot periodically sends status updates including its position, speed, and task progress.

- o The central coordinator should analyze this data to detect issues (e.g., delays, collisions, or failures).

2. Trigger Re-planning:

- o If a robot reports a failure or if an obstacle is detected, trigger a dynamic re-planning process.

- o Recalculate paths and reassign tasks as necessary.

- o Ensure that re-planning does not disrupt ongoing operations unnecessarily.

3. Implement Safety Protocols:

- o Integrate emergency stop mechanisms that can be triggered by the coordinator or individual robots in case of critical issues.

- o Maintain safe distances between robots to prevent collisions.

Step 5: Testing and Iteration

1. Simulate the Environment:

- o Before deploying on physical robots, test the coordination system in a simulated environment (e.g., Gazebo) to validate performance.

- o Identify and resolve issues related to communication delays, task allocation inaccuracies, or path planning inefficiencies.

2. **Deploy on Physical Robots:**

- o Once validated in simulation, deploy the coordination system on actual robots.

- o Monitor performance and gather data on task completion times, collision avoidance, and overall system efficiency.

3. **Iterate and Refine:**

- o Use feedback from tests to refine the task allocation algorithm, communication protocols, and path planning strategies.

- o Continuously update the system to handle new challenges and improve efficiency.

Diagram 4: Multi-Robot System Architecture

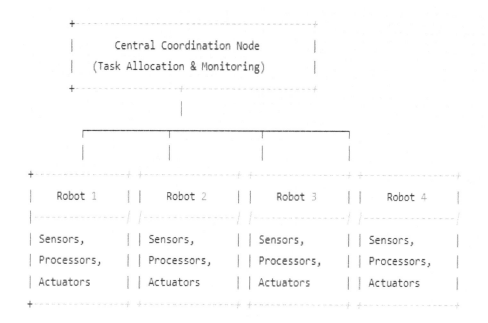

Description:

This diagram illustrates a vertical multi-robot system architecture where a central coordinator interacts with multiple robots. Each robot is depicted with its internal sensors and control modules, and communication links (topics, services, and actions) connect them to the central coordination node.

Summary

In **Chapter 8: Multi-Robot Coordination**, we embarked on a comprehensive journey into the world of collaborative robotics. Here's a recap of the key points covered:

   1. **Fundamentals of Multi-Robot Systems:**

- o **Benefits:** Increased efficiency, redundancy, scalability, and flexibility.

- o **Challenges:** Communication overhead, complex coordination algorithms, resource management, and interoperability.

- o **Diagram 1:** Multi-Robot System Architecture illustrated how a central coordinator interacts with individual robots.

2. **Communication Protocols:**

- o **Overview:** Explored topics, services, and actions as the building blocks for communication in multi-robot systems.

- o **Best Practices:** Minimizing latency, ensuring reliability, scalability, and security.

- o **Diagram 2:** Communication Protocols Overview provided a visual representation of these mechanisms.

3. **Cooperative Task Planning:**

- o **Strategies:** Task allocation (centralized vs. decentralized), scheduling, dynamic re-planning, and collision avoidance.

- o **Workflow:** A step-by-step process from task definition to execution and feedback.

- ○ **Diagram 3:** Task Planning Workflow depicted the sequential and iterative process of planning and execution.

4. **Hands-On Project: Coordinating a Team of Robots for a Common Task:**

   - ○ **Project Objectives:** Efficient collaboration, robust communication, adaptive task planning, and real-time control.

   - ○ **Step-by-Step Implementation:** From establishing a communication framework to dynamic re-planning and testing in both simulation and real-world environments.

With these strategies and tools at your disposal, you're now ready to harness the power of multi-robot coordination to tackle complex tasks that a single robot could never manage alone.

Next Steps: Control Systems and Actuation

With a robust multi-robot coordination framework in place, the next frontier is **Control Systems and Actuation.** In the upcoming chapter, we will explore how to precisely control robot movements, implement advanced actuation mechanisms, and integrate control algorithms that ensure smooth, coordinated operations. This will further enhance the capabilities of your multi-robot systems, ensuring they perform with accuracy and responsiveness.

Final Encouragement

Coordinating a team of robots is akin to conducting a symphony where every instrument must play in harmony to create a masterpiece. As you implement these strategies and integrate these systems, remember that the key to success is continuous learning, experimentation, and refinement. Each challenge you overcome will not only improve your system but also bring you closer to realizing truly autonomous, collaborative robotic operations. Stay curious, stay innovative, and keep pushing the boundaries of what's possible in robotics.

Happy coordinating, and here's to building the next generation of intelligent, multi-robot systems!

Chapter 9: Real-World Applications

Welcome to **Chapter 9: Real-World Applications**—the chapter where theory meets practice. In this section, we explore how autonomous robotics is not only a fascinating area of research but also a transformative technology that is reshaping industries and everyday life. From self-driving vehicles revolutionizing transportation to healthcare robots assisting in surgery and rehabilitation, and industrial automation streamlining manufacturing processes, the applications are vast and varied. This chapter will provide you with a deep dive into these applications, enriched with diagrams, step-by-step explanations, and real-world case studies that illustrate both successes and lessons learned.

Autonomous Vehicles

Robotics in Transportation and Logistics

Imagine a future where your car drives you to work while you catch up on emails, and trucks coordinate routes to deliver goods seamlessly across the country. Autonomous vehicles are at the forefront of this revolution, leveraging robotics and artificial intelligence to transform transportation and logistics.

What Are Autonomous Vehicles?

Autonomous vehicles (AVs) are vehicles capable of navigating and operating without human intervention. They combine sensor data, advanced algorithms, and real-time decision-making to drive safely and efficiently. AVs incorporate a myriad of robotics components, including:

- **LIDAR and Radar Sensors:** Provide a 360-degree view of the environment.

- **Cameras:** Capture visual data for object detection and recognition.

- **GPS and IMU:** Offer precise localization and orientation.

- **Control Systems:** Execute driving maneuvers such as acceleration, braking, and steering.

Key Benefits

1. **Safety Improvements:**

   - **Reduction in Human Error:** Autonomous systems can process information faster and react more consistently than human drivers.

   - **Accident Prevention:** Continuous monitoring and precise control help prevent collisions.

2. **Efficiency and Productivity:**

- ○ **Optimized Traffic Flow:** AVs can communicate with each other to reduce congestion and improve travel times.

- ○ **Reduced Fuel Consumption:** Efficient driving patterns lead to lower energy usage.

3. **Accessibility:**

- ○ **Mobility for All:** Autonomous vehicles can provide transportation options for those unable to drive, such as the elderly or disabled.

4. **Economic Impact:**

- ○ **Lower Operational Costs:** Reduced need for human drivers translates to significant cost savings.

- ○ **Enhanced Logistics:** Improved coordination in delivery systems boosts productivity across supply chains.

Challenges and Considerations

- **Regulatory Hurdles:** Establishing safety standards and legal frameworks for autonomous vehicles is complex.

- **Technological Limitations:** Ensuring reliable operation in diverse weather and road conditions remains a challenge.

- **Cybersecurity:** AVs must be protected against hacking and malicious attacks.

Healthcare Robotics

Applications in Surgery, Rehabilitation, and Assistance

Healthcare is one of the most transformative domains for robotics. Imagine a surgeon performing minimally invasive procedures with enhanced precision or a rehabilitation robot assisting patients to regain mobility. Robotics in healthcare is reshaping patient care by improving outcomes, reducing recovery times, and enhancing the overall quality of care.

Key Areas of Application

1. **Surgical Robotics:**

   o **Precision and Control:** Robotic surgical systems enable surgeons to perform complex procedures with greater accuracy and minimal invasiveness.

   o **Enhanced Visualization:** High-definition cameras and advanced imaging techniques provide surgeons with detailed views of the surgical site.

   o **Reduced Recovery Time:** Minimally invasive surgeries lead to shorter hospital stays and quicker patient recovery.

2. **Rehabilitation Robotics:**

- o **Personalized Therapy:** Robots can deliver consistent, personalized rehabilitation exercises tailored to each patient's needs.

- o **Continuous Monitoring:** Integrated sensors track patient progress and adjust therapy in real-time.

- o **Improved Motivation:** Interactive robotic systems can engage patients, making rehabilitation exercises more enjoyable.

3. **Assistive Robotics:**

- o **Elderly Care:** Robots can assist with daily tasks, ensuring safety and independence for the elderly.

- o **Disability Support:** Assistive devices help individuals with disabilities perform routine activities, enhancing their quality of life.

- o **Remote Healthcare:** Telepresence robots allow healthcare providers to monitor and interact with patients remotely.

Challenges in Healthcare Robotics

- **Regulatory Compliance:** Ensuring robotic systems meet stringent healthcare standards and safety regulations.

- **Cost and Accessibility:** Balancing advanced technology with affordability for widespread adoption.

- **Ethical Considerations:** Addressing concerns about patient privacy, autonomy, and the role of human caregivers.

Diagram 1: Healthcare Robotics Use Cases

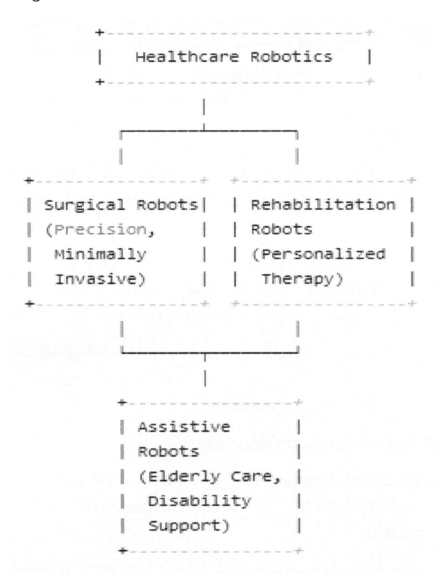

Description:

This diagram illustrates various use cases for healthcare robotics. It visually represents how surgical robots, rehabilitation devices, and assistive robots operate in different healthcare scenarios. Each block highlights key benefits, such as precision in surgery, personalized rehabilitation, and enhanced patient care in assistive applications.

Manufacturing and Industrial Automation

Enhancing Productivity with Autonomous Systems

Manufacturing and industrial automation have been revolutionized by robotics, leading to significant gains in productivity, quality, and efficiency. Imagine a factory where robots work in perfect harmony, assembling products with precision, maintaining equipment proactively, and adapting to changes in production demands—all without human intervention.

Key Applications

1. **Assembly Line Automation:**

- o **Consistent Quality:** Robots perform repetitive tasks with high precision, reducing variability and errors.

- o **Increased Throughput:** Automation speeds up production, enabling factories to meet high demand.

- o **Worker Safety:** Robots handle dangerous or strenuous tasks, reducing workplace injuries.

2. **Logistics and Material Handling:**

- o **Automated Warehousing:** Autonomous mobile robots (AMRs) streamline inventory management and order fulfillment.

- o **Optimized Routing:** Robots navigate efficiently within warehouses, reducing transit times and energy consumption.

- o **Scalability:** Systems can be expanded with additional robots without major overhauls.

3. **Predictive Maintenance:**

- o **Data-Driven Decisions:** Robots equipped with sensors continuously monitor machinery to predict and prevent failures.

- o **Reduced Downtime:** Timely maintenance minimizes unexpected breakdowns and production halts.

- ○ **Cost Savings:** Proactive maintenance reduces repair costs and extends equipment lifespan.

4. **Quality Control:**

   - ○ **Automated Inspection:** Vision systems and sensors detect defects in products, ensuring only high-quality items move forward.

   - ○ **Real-Time Feedback:** Continuous monitoring allows for immediate corrective actions, maintaining consistent quality.

Challenges and Considerations

- **Integration Complexity:** Incorporating robotics into existing production lines can be challenging.

- **Initial Investment:** High upfront costs can be a barrier for small and medium enterprises.

- **Workforce Transition:** Ensuring that the workforce adapts to new roles as automation increases.

- **Interoperability:** Seamlessly integrating robots from different manufacturers requires standardized protocols.

Diagram 2: Industrial Automation Processes

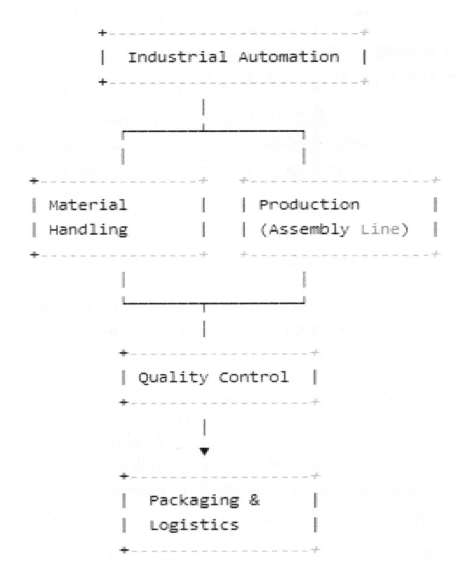

Description:

This diagram visualizes the industrial automation process in manufacturing. It illustrates the sequential flow from raw material handling to production, quality control, and packaging, highlighting how autonomous systems work at each stage to enhance productivity and efficiency.

Case Studies

Success Stories and Lessons Learned

Real-world applications of robotics provide valuable insights into both successes and challenges. In this section, we explore a few case studies that illustrate how autonomous systems have been implemented effectively, as well as the lessons learned along the way.

Case Study 1: Autonomous Vehicles in Urban Transportation

Overview:
A leading automotive company deployed a fleet of autonomous shuttles in a smart city pilot project. The vehicles navigated urban environments, dynamically rerouted based on traffic data, and communicated with city infrastructure to optimize routes.

Successes:

- **Improved Traffic Flow:** Real-time data integration reduced congestion significantly.

- **Enhanced Safety:** Automated driving systems reduced accidents attributed to human error.

- **Energy Efficiency:** Optimized routes lowered fuel consumption and emissions.

Lessons Learned:

- **Communication is Key:** Robust vehicle-to-everything (V2X) communication was critical for real-time adjustments.

- **Adaptive Algorithms:** Continuous learning and adaptation were essential for handling unpredictable urban scenarios.

- **Regulatory Hurdles:** Navigating legal and regulatory frameworks required close collaboration with city authorities.

Case Study 2: Surgical Robotics in Healthcare

Overview:

A major hospital implemented a robotic surgery system to assist with minimally invasive procedures. The system featured advanced imaging, precision control, and real-time feedback, allowing surgeons to perform complex operations with enhanced accuracy.

Successes:

- **Precision and Consistency:** The robotic system significantly reduced the margin of error during surgeries.

- **Shorter Recovery Times:** Patients benefited from less invasive procedures, resulting in faster recoveries.

- **Expanded Capabilities:** Surgeons were able to perform operations that were previously considered too risky.

Lessons Learned:

- **User Training:** Comprehensive training for surgeons was crucial for successful adoption.

- **Integration with Existing Systems:** Seamless integration with hospital IT and imaging systems was necessary.

- **Patient Safety:** Rigorous testing and certification ensured that the system met the highest safety standards.

Case Study 3: Robotic Automation in Manufacturing

Overview:
A global manufacturing firm revolutionized its production line by deploying a network of collaborative robots (cobots) on the assembly floor. These robots worked alongside human operators, handling repetitive tasks and allowing workers to focus on quality control and innovation.

Successes:

- **Increased Throughput:** Production rates increased by 40% without compromising quality.

- **Worker Safety:** Hazardous tasks were automated, reducing workplace injuries.

- **Cost Savings:** Operational costs dropped significantly due to higher efficiency and lower error rates.

Lessons Learned:

- **Change Management:** Transitioning the workforce to work with robots required careful planning and communication.

- **Interoperability:** Standardized communication protocols facilitated smooth collaboration between robots from different vendors.

- **Scalability:** The modular nature of the robotic system allowed for gradual scaling without major disruptions.

Summary

In **Chapter 9: Real-World Applications**, we've navigated through the transformative landscape of autonomous robotics in various sectors:

1. **Autonomous Vehicles:**
   - **Overview:** Explored how robotics is revolutionizing transportation and logistics.
   - **Benefits:** Improved safety, efficiency, accessibility, and reduced operational costs.

2. **Healthcare Robotics:**
   - **Overview:** Examined how robotics enhances surgical precision, rehabilitation, and assistive care.
   - **Benefits:** Enhanced patient outcomes, reduced recovery times, and increased efficiency.

- o **Diagram 1:** Visualized use cases in healthcare robotics, delineating applications in surgery, rehabilitation, and assistive environments.

3. **Manufacturing and Industrial Automation:**

   - o **Overview:** Detailed how autonomous systems boost productivity and safety in manufacturing.

   - o **Benefits:** Increased throughput, reduced costs, and improved worker safety.

   - o **Diagram 2:** Illustrated industrial automation processes from material handling through production to packaging.

4. **Case Studies:**

   - o **Success Stories and Lessons Learned:** Shared real-world examples from autonomous vehicles, healthcare, and industrial automation, highlighting both achievements and the challenges encountered.

These applications showcase not only the technological prowess of modern robotics but also their profound impact on industries and society. By integrating advanced robotics into these sectors, we are not only increasing efficiency but also paving the way for safer, more innovative, and sustainable future solutions.

Next Steps: Control Systems and Actuation

With an understanding of real-world applications, you're now ready to tackle the next challenge: **Control Systems and Actuation.** In the upcoming chapter, we'll explore how to precisely control robot movements, implement advanced actuation mechanisms, and integrate control algorithms to ensure smooth, accurate execution of tasks. This will further empower your robotic systems, bringing the full spectrum of autonomous capabilities to life.

Final Encouragement

The journey through real-world applications of robotics is both inspiring and humbling. From the high-speed precision of autonomous vehicles to the delicate balance of healthcare robotics and the robust efficiency of industrial automation, these technologies are reshaping our world. As you continue your exploration, remember that every challenge is an opportunity to innovate and improve. Stay curious, embrace complexity, and let your passion for robotics drive you to build solutions that not only work but also transform industries and lives.

Happy innovating!

Chapter 10: Troubleshooting and Optimization

Welcome to **Chapter 10: Troubleshooting and Optimization**—the ultimate guide to diagnosing and fine-tuning your robotics projects for peak performance. Even the most well-designed systems encounter issues. Whether it's a sensor misalignment, a sluggish response time, or an unexpected error in communication between nodes, the ability to troubleshoot and optimize is essential. This chapter is designed to equip you with the tools, techniques, and best practices to identify common challenges, enhance performance, and debug your system effectively. We'll cover common robotics issues, performance optimization strategies, and debugging methodologies, culminating in a hands-on project to optimize your autonomous robot. Let's dive into the world of troubleshooting and optimization like a seasoned tech pro!

Common Challenges in Robotics Projects

Identifying and Addressing Typical Issues

Every robotics project, no matter how meticulously planned, is bound to face challenges. These issues can range from hardware malfunctions to software bugs, communication delays to sensor inaccuracies. Recognizing these common pitfalls is the first step toward building a robust and reliable robotic system.

Typical Issues in Robotics

1. **Sensor Inaccuracies:**

   o **Drift and Noise:** Sensors like IMUs and LIDAR may produce noisy or drifting data, which can affect localization and mapping.

   o **Calibration Errors:** Misaligned or improperly calibrated sensors can lead to inaccurate readings.

2. **Communication Latency:**

   o **Delayed Data Transmission:** Network congestion or inefficient middleware configurations can slow down communication between nodes.

- ○ **Packet Loss:** In wireless networks, packet loss may occur, leading to incomplete or corrupted data.

3. **Software Bugs:**

   - ○ **Memory Leaks:** Inefficient resource management can cause memory leaks, resulting in system slowdowns or crashes.

   - ○ **Logic Errors:** Flaws in algorithms or incorrect state transitions can lead to unpredictable behavior.

4. **Hardware Failures:**

   - ○ **Actuator Malfunctions:** Motors and servos might fail or degrade over time, impacting the robot's ability to move accurately.

   - ○ **Power Supply Issues:** Insufficient or unstable power can lead to erratic performance.

5. **Integration Challenges:**

   - ○ **Interoperability Issues:** Combining components from different vendors can result in compatibility issues.

   - ○ **Complex Dependencies:** Managing dependencies between software packages can be a headache, especially when updates or changes are introduced.

Best Practices for Addressing Common Challenges

- **Regular Calibration:** Schedule periodic calibration of sensors to ensure accuracy.

- **Redundant Systems:** Incorporate redundancy in critical components to enhance reliability.

- **Robust Communication:** Optimize network configurations and choose reliable communication protocols.

- **Code Reviews and Testing:** Implement rigorous testing, code reviews, and automated validation to catch bugs early.

- **Monitoring Tools:** Use system monitors to track resource usage, detect memory leaks, and log errors in real time.

Diagram 1: Common Robotics Issues

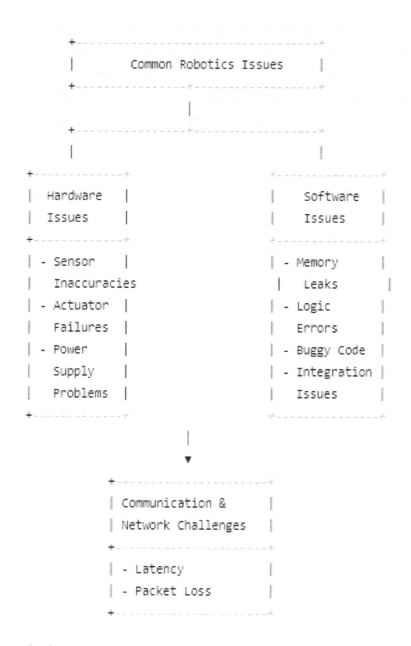

Description:

This diagram provides a visual summary of the typical challenges encountered in robotics projects. It categorizes issues into hardware, software, and integration challenges and illustrates the potential impacts of each on system performance.

Performance Optimization

Enhancing Speed, Efficiency, and Reliability

Optimizing your robotics system is not just about making it faster—it's about improving overall efficiency and ensuring reliable performance under diverse conditions. Performance optimization involves fine-tuning algorithms, streamlining code, and ensuring that the hardware and software components operate harmoniously.

Key Areas for Optimization

1. **Algorithm Optimization:**

    o **Efficient Path Planning:** Improve algorithms like A* or RRT to reduce computation time and energy consumption.

    o **Sensor Fusion:** Optimize data fusion techniques to obtain accurate and timely information from multiple sensors.

2. **Code Optimization:**

    o **Streamlined Logic:** Refactor code to remove redundancies and optimize critical sections.

- o **Memory Management:** Implement techniques to prevent memory leaks and optimize resource usage.

3. **Hardware Utilization:**

   - o **Parallel Processing:** Leverage multi-threading or asynchronous programming (e.g., Python's asyncio) to maximize CPU and GPU usage.

   - o **Power Efficiency:** Optimize the robot's power consumption by dynamically adjusting performance based on current tasks.

4. **Network Optimization:**

   - o **Latency Reduction:** Fine-tune network configurations and middleware settings to minimize communication delays.

   - o **Data Compression:** Use efficient data encoding and compression methods to reduce the bandwidth required for sensor data.

5. **System-Level Optimization:**

   - o **Feedback Loops:** Implement continuous monitoring and real-time feedback to adjust performance on the fly.

   - o **Profiling and Benchmarking:** Regularly profile your system to identify bottlenecks and measure improvements.

Strategies for Optimization

- **Profiling Tools:** Use tools like ROS2's built-in profilers, Python's cProfile, and hardware monitoring software.

- **Iterative Refinement:** Continuously test and refine both software and hardware components.

- **Load Balancing:** Distribute computational tasks evenly across available processors.

- **Simulation Testing:** Validate changes in simulation environments before deploying them on real hardware.

Diagram 2: Optimization Techniques

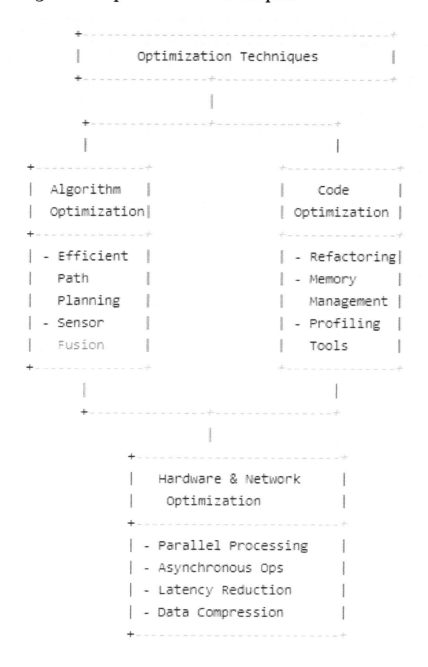

Description:

This diagram illustrates various optimization techniques that can be applied to robotics systems. It outlines strategies for algorithmic improvements, code refactoring, hardware utilization, and network optimization. Each category includes examples of specific techniques and tools used for performance enhancement.

Debugging Techniques

Tools and Methodologies for Effective Troubleshooting

Even the most optimized systems encounter errors, and debugging is an essential skill for any robotics engineer. Effective debugging involves identifying the root causes of issues, testing potential solutions, and iterating until the system operates flawlessly. Whether you're dealing with intermittent sensor glitches or complex logic errors in your code, a systematic approach to debugging can save time and enhance system reliability.

Essential Debugging Tools

1. **Logging:**

    o **Description:** Systematically record events and errors to track system behavior.

    o **Best Practices:** Use various log levels (DEBUG, INFO, WARN, ERROR) to filter messages and focus on critical issues.

2. **Profiling Tools:**

- o **cProfile and ROS2 Profilers:** Identify performance bottlenecks by analyzing the time spent in various parts of your code.

- o **Visualization:** Tools like KCachegrind can help visualize profiling data.

3. **Simulation Environments:**

- o **Gazebo:** Test your system in a simulated environment to replicate real-world scenarios.

- o **RViz2:** Visualize sensor data, robot states, and debug messages in real time.

4. **Network Analysis Tools:**

- o **Wireshark:** Monitor and analyze network traffic to diagnose communication issues.

- o **Ping and Traceroute:** Check connectivity and latency between network nodes.

5. **Integrated Development Environments (IDEs):**

- o **Visual Studio Code, PyCharm:** Use breakpoints, step-through debugging, and variable inspection to diagnose issues in your code.

Methodologies for Effective Debugging

1. **Divide and Conquer:**

- o Break down the system into individual modules and test each component separately.

- o Identify which module or interaction is causing the issue.

2. **Reproduce the Error:**
   - o Try to recreate the error consistently in a controlled environment.
   - o Document the conditions under which the error occurs.

3. **Incremental Testing:**
   - o Test changes incrementally and verify their impact on system performance.
   - o Use unit tests and integration tests to ensure that fixes do not introduce new issues.

4. **Hypothesis and Experiment:**
   - o Formulate hypotheses about the source of the problem and design experiments to test them.
   - o Use data and logs to validate your assumptions.

5. **Peer Review:**
   - o Collaborate with team members to review code and system designs.
   - o Fresh perspectives can often spot issues that you might have missed.

Diagram 3: Debugging Workflow

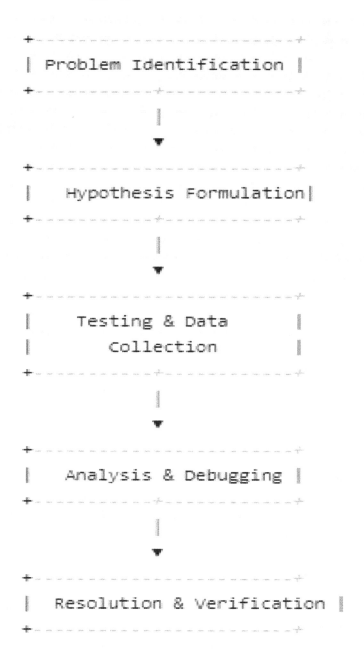

Description:

This diagram visualizes a typical debugging workflow for robotics systems. It outlines the process from problem identification, through hypothesis formation, testing, analysis, and finally resolution. The workflow emphasizes iterative testing and continuous feedback.

Hands-On Project: Optimizing Your Autonomous Robot

Project Overview

In this hands-on project, you'll put all these troubleshooting and optimization techniques into practice by optimizing your autonomous robot. The goal is to identify performance bottlenecks, resolve issues, and fine-tune the system to enhance speed, efficiency, and reliability. You'll work through a systematic process that involves:

- **Identifying common issues:** Using logs and profiling tools.

- **Applying optimization techniques:** Refining algorithms, streamlining code, and improving communication.

- **Implementing robust debugging strategies:** Using simulation and real-world testing to validate your improvements.

- **Iterating until performance goals are met.**

Step-by-Step Guide

Step 1: System Profiling and Issue Identification

1. **Enable Detailed Logging:**

   - Configure your ROS2 nodes to log at the DEBUG level.

   - Use commands like:

bash

Copy

ros2 run your_package your_node --ros-args --log-level DEBUG

2. **Run Profiling Tools:**

   - Utilize Python's cProfile or ROS2 performance analyzers to collect data on CPU and memory usage.

   - Document the time taken for critical operations such as sensor data processing and path planning.

3. **Identify Bottlenecks:**

   - Analyze logs and profiler outputs to pinpoint slow or error-prone sections.

   - List common issues like delayed sensor data, slow decision-making loops, or high memory consumption.

Step 2: Applying Optimization Techniques

1. **Refactor Critical Code Sections:**

   o Optimize algorithms by reducing unnecessary computations.

   o Consider rewriting performance-critical sections in a compiled language if needed.

2. **Implement Asynchronous Operations:**

   o Where possible, convert blocking operations to asynchronous ones using Python's asyncio.

   o Test the system to ensure that asynchronous execution improves responsiveness.

3. **Improve Resource Management:**

   o Implement proper memory management practices to prevent leaks.

   o Use garbage collection tuning and optimize data structures for speed.

4. **Optimize Communication:**

   o Tune ROS2 middleware settings to reduce latency.

   o Implement data compression techniques where high bandwidth usage is identified.

Step 3: Debugging and Iterative Testing

1. **Set Breakpoints and Monitor Variables:**

- o Use an IDE to set breakpoints in critical sections of your code.
- o Monitor variable values to ensure they are within expected ranges.

2. **Use Simulation Environments:**

- o Test your optimizations in Gazebo or RViz2 to visualize the effects.
- o Adjust parameters based on real-time feedback.

3. **Conduct A/B Testing:**

- o Compare the performance of the optimized system against the baseline.
- o Document improvements in speed, efficiency, and reliability.

4. **Collect and Analyze Feedback:**

- o Solicit feedback from team members or operators.
- o Use logs to verify that issues have been resolved and performance goals are met.

Step 4: Final Integration and Deployment

1. **Integrate All Optimizations:**

- o Combine the optimized modules into the main system.

- o Ensure that changes in one module do not adversely affect another.

2. **Deploy on the Physical Robot:**

   - o Test the integrated system in a real-world environment.

   - o Monitor performance and make final adjustments as needed.

3. **Document the Process:**

   - o Maintain detailed records of the issues encountered, optimizations applied, and results achieved.

   - o Use this documentation as a reference for future troubleshooting efforts.

Summary

In **Chapter 10: Troubleshooting and Optimization**, we've explored the critical aspects of ensuring that your robotics projects run smoothly and efficiently. Here's a quick recap:

1. **Common Challenges in Robotics Projects:**

   - o **Identification and Resolution:** We discussed typical issues such as sensor inaccuracies, communication delays, software bugs, and hardware failures.

- ○ **Diagram 1:** A visual representation of common robotics issues, categorizing them into hardware, software, and network challenges.

2. **Performance Optimization:**

   - ○ **Strategies and Best Practices:** Detailed techniques to enhance algorithm efficiency, streamline code, manage resources, and optimize network communication.

   - ○ **Diagram 2:** A diagram outlining various optimization techniques across algorithmic, code, and hardware/network levels.

3. **Debugging Techniques:**

   - ○ **Tools and Methodologies:** Covered logging, profiling, simulation, network analysis, and the use of IDE debuggers.

   - ○ **Diagram 3:** A debugging workflow that visualizes the iterative process from problem identification to resolution and verification.

4. **Hands-On Project: Optimizing Your Autonomous Robot:**

   - ○ **Step-by-Step Process:** From profiling and issue identification to applying optimizations and final integration, you learned how to systematically enhance your robot's performance.

These strategies and techniques not only help you troubleshoot and resolve issues but also empower you to continuously refine and enhance your robotics projects for greater speed, efficiency, and reliability.

Final Encouragement

Troubleshooting and optimization are integral to the lifecycle of any robotics project. The ability to diagnose problems, implement efficient solutions, and continuously improve your system is what separates good projects from great ones. Embrace the iterative process, remain persistent in the face of challenges, and let every setback be an opportunity for learning and innovation. Your commitment to excellence is the key to building reliable, high-performance robotic systems. Happy debugging and optimizing!

Chapter 11: Future Trends in Autonomous Robotics

Welcome to **Chapter 11: Future Trends in Autonomous Robotics**—your gateway to what lies ahead in this dynamic field. As we stand on the brink of a technological revolution, autonomous robotics is evolving at an unprecedented pace. In this chapter, we explore emerging technologies, ethical considerations, and the future workforce that will drive these innovations forward. We'll also walk through a hands-on project that invites you to experiment with these future trends using a prototype. Get ready to peer into the future and discover how advancements in artificial intelligence, edge computing, and more are set to transform the robotics landscape.

Emerging Technologies

AI Advancements, Edge Computing, and Beyond

Imagine a world where robots are not only self-navigating but also capable of making split-second decisions based on real-time data analysis—all while operating independently at the edge of networks. This is the future of autonomous robotics, where emerging technologies are converging to create systems that are smarter, faster, and more resilient.

Artificial Intelligence and Machine Learning

At the heart of future robotics is artificial intelligence (AI). Recent advancements in AI are enabling robots to process vast amounts of data and learn from their environments with unprecedented efficiency. Key developments include:

- **Deep Learning and Neural Networks:**
  Modern deep learning architectures such as convolutional neural networks (CNNs), recurrent neural networks (RNNs), and transformers are dramatically improving the accuracy of perception systems. These models enable robots to recognize complex patterns, identify objects in cluttered environments, and even predict future events based on historical data.

- **Reinforcement Learning (RL):**
  Reinforcement learning has evolved to power decision-making processes in robots. By learning through trial and error and receiving rewards for optimal behavior, RL algorithms enable robots to develop sophisticated strategies for navigation, manipulation, and multi-robot coordination.

- **Federated Learning:**
  Federated learning allows multiple robots to collaboratively train a shared model while keeping data locally on each device. This approach enhances privacy, reduces the need for central data storage, and

allows robots to learn from diverse environments without sharing raw data.

Edge Computing

While cloud computing has traditionally been the powerhouse for processing large datasets, the future of robotics is moving towards **edge computing**. Here's why:

- **Reduced Latency:**
  By processing data locally on the robot (or on nearby edge devices), robots can make decisions in real time without the delays associated with transmitting data to a distant data center.

- **Enhanced Privacy and Security:**
  Local data processing minimizes the risk of data breaches, ensuring that sensitive information remains on the device.

- **Scalability and Robustness:**
  Edge computing enables systems to operate independently of continuous cloud connectivity, making robots more robust in environments with poor or intermittent network access.

Other Emerging Technologies

In addition to AI and edge computing, several other technologies are set to revolutionize autonomous robotics:

- **Quantum Computing:**
  Although still in its infancy, quantum computing

promises to solve complex optimization and simulation problems far more quickly than classical computers. For robotics, this could mean more efficient path planning and decision-making processes.

- **5G and Beyond:**
  The rollout of 5G networks, with its high bandwidth and ultra-low latency, will support real-time communication between robots, enabling seamless coordination in multi-robot systems.

- **Advanced Sensors and Actuators:**
  The continuous improvement in sensor technologies—such as high-resolution LIDAR, thermal cameras, and novel bio-inspired sensors—will enhance a robot's ability to perceive its environment. Similarly, advances in actuator technology will lead to smoother, more precise movements.

- **Digital Twins:**
  Digital twin technology creates virtual replicas of physical robotic systems, enabling simulation, monitoring, and predictive maintenance in real time. This can dramatically improve system reliability and performance.

Ethical Considerations

Ensuring Responsible Development and Deployment

As robotics become increasingly autonomous and integrated into society, ethical considerations are paramount. Ensuring that these advanced systems are developed and deployed responsibly is not just a technical challenge—it's a societal imperative.

Key Ethical Issues in Robotics

1. **Privacy and Data Security:**

   o **Data Collection:** Autonomous robots often gather vast amounts of data from their environments. Ensuring that this data is handled securely and ethically is crucial.

   o **Consent and Transparency:** Users must be informed about what data is being collected and how it is used.

2. **Bias and Fairness:**

   o **Algorithmic Bias:** AI models can inadvertently learn and propagate biases present in training data, leading to unfair or discriminatory outcomes.

- o **Equal Access:** Ensuring that advancements in robotics benefit all segments of society without exacerbating existing inequalities.

3. **Safety and Accountability:**

   - o **Fail-Safe Mechanisms:** Autonomous systems must include robust safety protocols to prevent accidents and unintended behavior.

   - o **Liability:** Determining accountability when an autonomous system fails is complex. Clear legal frameworks are needed to address liability.

4. **Job Displacement and Workforce Impact:**

   - o **Automation Effects:** While robotics can enhance productivity, they may also displace certain job roles. Society must address the implications of automation on employment.

   - o **Reskilling and Education:** There should be initiatives to help workers transition to new roles that leverage advanced technologies.

5. **Autonomy vs. Control:**

   - o **Human Oversight:** Striking the right balance between autonomous decision-making and human control is essential to ensure that robots act in the best interests of society.

- ○ **Ethical AI:** Developing AI systems that align with human values and ethical principles is a critical challenge.

Best Practices for Ethical Robotics

- **Transparent Design:** Develop systems with clear documentation and open communication about how data is used and how decisions are made.

- **Inclusive Data Practices:** Use diverse and representative datasets to train AI models, minimizing the risk of bias.

- **Safety Protocols:** Implement robust safety measures and regularly audit systems to ensure compliance with ethical standards.

- **Stakeholder Engagement:** Involve ethicists, policymakers, and the public in the development process to address societal concerns.

- **Regulatory Compliance:** Adhere to emerging regulations and standards for robotics and AI.

Diagram 1: Ethics in Robotics

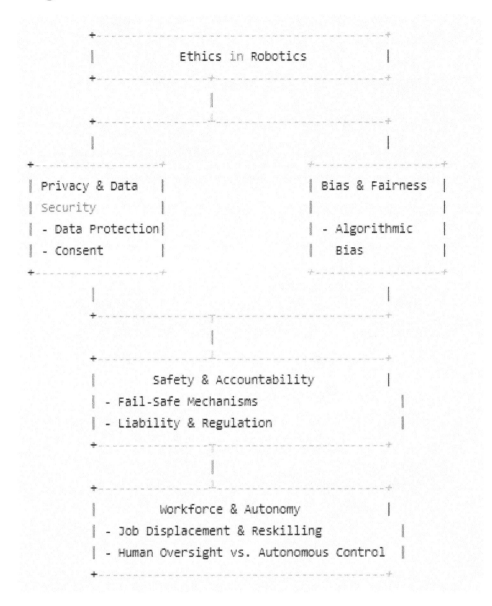

Description:

This diagram highlights the key ethical considerations in robotics. It categorizes ethical issues into areas such as Privacy & Data Security, Bias & Fairness, Safety & Accountability, Job Displacement, and Autonomy vs.

Control. The diagram uses icons and labels to visually represent each ethical domain and illustrates the interconnected nature of these concerns.

The Future Workforce

Skills and Knowledge for Upcoming Robotics Professionals

As robotics continues to evolve, so too does the demand for a highly skilled workforce that can design, build, and maintain these advanced systems. The future workforce in autonomous robotics will require a unique blend of technical expertise, creative problem-solving, and ethical awareness.

Key Skills for the Future

1. **Advanced Programming and AI:**
   - **Proficiency in Python and C++:** Essential for developing and optimizing robotic systems.
   - **Machine Learning and Deep Learning:** Understanding AI models and their applications in robotics is critical.
   - **Algorithm Design:** The ability to develop efficient algorithms for perception, navigation, and control.

2. Systems Engineering:

- o **Integration Skills:** Knowledge of how to integrate hardware and software components seamlessly.

- o **Real-Time Systems:** Experience with real-time processing, communication protocols, and system optimization.

- o **Simulation and Modeling:** Proficiency in using simulation tools like Gazebo and RViz2 to test and validate designs.

3. Data Analytics and Cybersecurity:

- o **Data Handling:** Skills in managing, processing, and analyzing large datasets from various sensors.

- o **Cybersecurity:** Understanding how to secure robotic systems against potential threats is increasingly important.

4. Interdisciplinary Collaboration:

- o **Teamwork:** The ability to work in multidisciplinary teams, integrating knowledge from computer science, engineering, and ethics.

- o **Communication:** Strong communication skills to articulate complex ideas to diverse stakeholders.

- ○ **Ethical and Social Awareness:** Understanding the societal impacts of robotics and the ethical considerations involved.

Educational Pathways

- **Formal Education:** Degrees in robotics, computer science, electrical engineering, and related fields remain fundamental.

- **Bootcamps and Workshops:** Intensive training programs can rapidly upskill professionals in the latest robotics technologies.

- **Online Courses and Certifications:** Platforms like Coursera, edX, and Udacity offer specialized courses in robotics, AI, and machine learning.

- **Hands-On Projects:** Real-world projects and internships provide invaluable experience and practical knowledge.

Hands-On Project: Exploring Future Trends with a Prototype

Project Overview

In this hands-on project, you will explore future trends in autonomous robotics by developing a prototype that integrates emerging technologies, addresses ethical considerations, and demonstrates the advanced skills required for the future workforce. This project is designed to be both experimental and practical, allowing you to test cutting-edge ideas and assess their feasibility in a real-world scenario.

Project Objectives

1. **Integrate Emerging Technologies:**
   - Combine AI advancements and edge computing to create a smart, autonomous system.
   - Implement advanced sensor fusion and data processing techniques.

2. **Address Ethical Considerations:**
   - Ensure data privacy and system transparency in the prototype.
   - Develop ethical guidelines for the prototype's operation.

3. **Showcase Future Workforce Skills:**
   - Demonstrate advanced programming, system integration, and real-time data processing.
   - Highlight interdisciplinary collaboration through the prototype's design and implementation.

4. **Real-World Performance:**
   - Optimize the prototype for speed, efficiency, and reliability.

  ○ Validate the system's performance through simulation and physical testing.

Step-by-Step Project Guide

Step 1: Define the Project Scope

- **Objective:** Develop a prototype autonomous system capable of navigating an environment using AI and edge computing.

- **Requirements:** Identify the key components (sensors, processing unit, communication modules) and specify performance metrics (latency, accuracy, energy efficiency).

Step 2: Hardware and Software Setup

- **Select Hardware:** Choose an appropriate robotic platform (e.g., a TurtleBot3 or a custom-built robot) equipped with advanced sensors (LIDAR, cameras) and a capable onboard computer (e.g., NVIDIA Jetson).

- **Install ROS2 and Dependencies:** Ensure your development environment is configured with ROS2 and necessary libraries (TensorFlow, PyTorch, OpenCV).

Step 3: Integrate Emerging Technologies

- **AI and Edge Computing:**

- o Develop a module that uses edge computing to process sensor data in real time.

- o Integrate a deep learning model for object detection or navigation (e.g., using YOLO or a CNN).

- **Data Fusion:**

  - o Implement sensor fusion algorithms to combine data from multiple sources (e.g., LIDAR and camera).

  - o Ensure that the system processes data efficiently and reliably.

Step 4: Implement Ethical Safeguards

- **Data Privacy:**

  - o Design the system to process sensitive data locally, minimizing the need for external data transfers.

  - o Implement secure data handling practices and anonymization where necessary.

- **Transparency and Accountability:**

  - o Develop logging and reporting mechanisms that provide clear insights into the system's decision-making processes.

  - o Create a user interface that displays system status and ethical guidelines for operation.

Step 5: Develop the Prototype

- **Coding and Integration:**
    - Write modular code for each subsystem (sensor processing, AI inference, communication, control).
    - Use ROS2 nodes to integrate the subsystems, ensuring smooth communication between components.

- **Simulation Testing:**
    - Deploy the prototype in a simulated environment using tools like Gazebo and RViz2.
    - Validate functionality, performance, and ethical safeguards in a controlled setting.

Step 6: Real-World Deployment and Iteration

- **Physical Testing:**
    - Once the prototype performs well in simulation, deploy it on the physical robot.
    - Monitor its performance in real-world scenarios and gather feedback.

- **Optimization and Refinement:**
    - Use performance profiling tools and debugging techniques to fine-tune the system.

- o Iterate based on real-world data, enhancing AI models, optimizing sensor fusion, and improving communication.

Step 7: Documentation and Presentation

- **Document the Process:**
    - o Keep detailed records of your development process, challenges encountered, and solutions implemented.
    - o Create a project report that outlines the system architecture, integration of emerging technologies, ethical safeguards, and performance metrics.

- **Showcase Your Prototype:**
    - o Prepare a presentation or demonstration of your prototype to highlight its capabilities and potential impact.
    - o Discuss the future trends reflected in your project and the skills needed to drive these advancements.

Summary

In **Chapter 11: Future Trends in Autonomous Robotics**, we've embarked on a comprehensive exploration of what the future holds for this dynamic field. Here's a recap of the key points:

1. **Emerging Technologies:**

   - Explored advancements in AI, edge computing, quantum computing, and next-generation sensors.

2. **Ethical Considerations:**

   - Addressed the importance of data privacy, algorithmic fairness, safety, accountability, and workforce impacts.

   - **Diagram 1:** Illustrated key ethical domains in robotics, highlighting the balance between innovation and responsible development.

3. **The Future Workforce:**

   - Outlined the essential skills for upcoming robotics professionals, from advanced programming and AI to systems engineering and interdisciplinary collaboration.

4. **Hands-On Project:**

   - Provided a detailed, step-by-step guide to building a prototype that integrates emerging technologies, implements ethical safeguards, and showcases future workforce skills.

   - The project demonstrated how to leverage edge computing, deep learning, and sensor fusion to create an autonomous system ready for real-world challenges.

These insights not only prepare you for the future but also equip you with practical tools and methodologies to innovate and lead in the field of autonomous robotics.

Final Encouragement

The future of autonomous robotics is bright and full of potential. By embracing emerging technologies, adhering to ethical standards, and continually updating your skill set, you are at the forefront of a revolution that will reshape industries and improve lives. Keep experimenting, keep innovating, and never stop learning. Your journey into the future of robotics is just beginning—step boldly into it, and let your passion drive you to create systems that are as responsible as they are revolutionary.

Happy building, and here's to a future filled with intelligent, ethical, and groundbreaking robotic innovations!

Chapter 12: Capstone Project – Designing an Advanced Autonomous System

Welcome to the grand finale of your autonomous robotics journey—**the Capstone Project**. This is where you combine all the knowledge and skills you've acquired throughout the book to design, implement, test, and deploy an advanced autonomous system. Think of it as your opportunity to create a masterpiece, much like a seasoned architect brings together form, function, and aesthetics to design a cutting-edge building. In this chapter, we'll walk you through a comprehensive, step-by-step guide—from conception to execution—of building an advanced autonomous system. We'll cover system design, implementation strategies, testing protocols, and deployment tactics, supported by clear diagrams that illustrate each phase of the project.

Designing an Advanced Autonomous System

Integrating All Learned Concepts

By now, you have built a strong foundation in ROS2, Python programming, machine learning, sensor integration, path planning, multi-robot coordination, and more. The capstone project is where all these pieces come together. Your task is to design a fully functional autonomous system that can operate in a real-world environment. This system should be capable of perceiving its surroundings, making intelligent decisions, and executing tasks reliably.

Imagine an autonomous robot that can:

- **Sense:** Utilize LIDAR, cameras, and IMUs to perceive its environment.

- **Process:** Use advanced perception algorithms and machine learning to identify objects, plan routes, and adapt to changes.

- **Act:** Navigate through dynamic environments, perform collaborative tasks, and adjust its behavior in real time.

- **Communicate:** Interact with other robots or a central command unit for coordinated operations.

Key Design Objectives

1. **Robust Sensor Integration:**

- Seamlessly combine data from multiple sensors to create a comprehensive environmental model.

- Ensure accurate calibration and synchronization to minimize noise and drift.

2. **Advanced Perception and Decision-Making:**

- Implement deep learning models for object detection and scene understanding.

- Integrate reinforcement learning or traditional algorithms for dynamic decision-making.

3. **Efficient Path Planning and Navigation:**

- Use algorithms such as A^* or RRT for optimal route computation.

- Incorporate real-time re-planning to handle dynamic obstacles.

4. **Multi-Robot Coordination (Optional):**

- If working with a team of robots, design a communication framework that allows seamless task allocation and collaboration.

- Ensure robust inter-robot communication using ROS2 topics, services, and actions.

5. **User Interface and Feedback:**

- Develop a dashboard or visualization tool (using RViz2 or a custom web interface) to monitor system status, sensor data, and operational metrics.

o Implement logging and error reporting for continuous system improvement.

Diagram 1: Capstone Project Overview

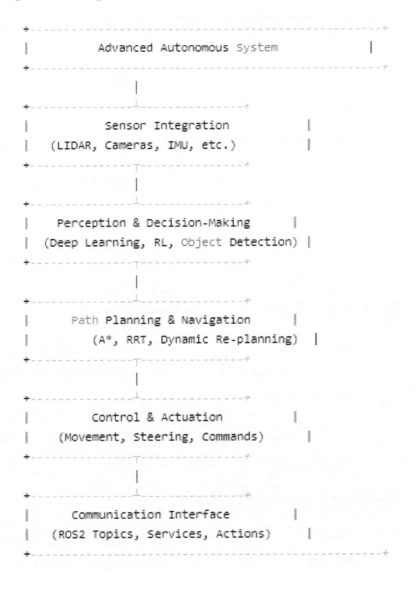

Description:

This diagram presents a high-level view of the advanced autonomous system you will design. It includes the main components: sensor integration, perception and decision-making, path planning and navigation, control systems, and communication interfaces. The diagram serves as a roadmap of how various subsystems interconnect to create a fully functional autonomous robot.

Step-by-Step Implementation

From Conception to Execution

Designing and building an advanced autonomous system is an iterative process that involves several key phases. Below, we break down the process into clear, actionable steps.

Step 1: Conception and Planning

1. **Define the Mission:**
   - **Objective:** Determine what the autonomous system should achieve. Examples include navigating a complex environment, performing object manipulation, or coordinating with other robots.
   - **Requirements:** Outline the technical specifications such as sensor types, processing power, communication protocols, and performance metrics.

2. **Sketch the System Architecture:**

   o Draw a preliminary diagram (like Diagram 1 above) that maps out all the subsystems and their interactions.

   o Identify the key modules: sensor integration, perception, path planning, control, and communication.

3. **Resource Allocation:**

   o **Hardware:** Select a robotic platform and the necessary sensors (e.g., LIDAR, cameras, IMU).

   o **Software:** Ensure you have the latest versions of ROS2, Python libraries, machine learning frameworks, and simulation tools installed.

4. **Risk Analysis:**

   o Identify potential challenges such as sensor noise, latency in decision-making, and communication failures.

   o Develop contingency plans to mitigate these risks.

Step 2: Component Development

1. **Sensor Integration Module:**

   o **Connect Sensors:** Mount and calibrate sensors on your robot.

- o **Develop ROS2 Nodes:** Write nodes to read sensor data and publish it on appropriate topics.

- o **Synchronize Data:** Implement time-stamping and data fusion techniques to ensure coherent environmental modeling.

2. **Perception and Decision-Making Module:**

- o **Implement Deep Learning Models:** Integrate object detection or scene classification models (e.g., YOLO, CNNs).

- o **Decision Algorithms:** Incorporate algorithms (like reinforcement learning or rule-based systems) to process sensor data and make navigation or task decisions.

- o **Testing:** Validate model accuracy using simulated data before deploying on real sensors.

3. **Path Planning and Navigation Module:**

- o **Develop Algorithms:** Implement A*, RRT, or other suitable algorithms for path computation.

- o **Dynamic Re-planning:** Ensure your module can adapt to changing environments by re-calculating paths in real time.

- o **Integration:** Connect the planning module with the perception system to receive continuous updates.

4. **Control and Actuation Module:**

- o **Movement Commands:** Develop ROS2 nodes to convert high-level navigation decisions into low-level actuator commands.

- o **Feedback Loops:** Integrate real-time feedback from sensors to adjust movement commands for accuracy and safety.

5. **Communication Interface:**

- o **Implement ROS2 Communication:** Use topics, services, and actions to ensure that all modules communicate seamlessly.

- o **Multi-Robot Consideration (Optional):** If coordinating multiple robots, set up a central controller and inter-robot communication protocols.

Step 3: Integration and Testing

1. **Integrate Components:**

- o Merge all the modules into a unified system.

- o Ensure that each ROS2 node communicates effectively with others.

2. **Simulation Testing:**

- o Use simulation tools like Gazebo and RViz2 to test your system in a virtual environment.

- o Validate sensor data integration, decision-making, path planning, and control.

- o Identify and resolve integration issues before moving to physical testing.

3. **Field Testing:**
   - o Deploy the system on the physical robot.
   - o Run comprehensive tests in real-world scenarios to validate performance, reliability, and safety.
   - o Monitor logs, sensor data, and robot behavior to ensure the system meets the defined objectives.

Step 4: Optimization and Iteration

1. **Performance Profiling:**
   - o Use profiling tools to measure the system's speed, latency, and resource usage.
   - o Identify bottlenecks in processing or communication.

2. **Optimization:**
   - o Refine algorithms and code for improved performance.
   - o Adjust sensor calibration and data fusion techniques.
   - o Optimize network configurations to reduce latency.

3. **Iterative Refinement:**

- o Continuously test and refine the system based on feedback and performance data.

- o Implement incremental updates and re-test to ensure stability.

Step 5: Documentation and Presentation

1. **Document the Process:**

   - o Maintain detailed records of design decisions, challenges encountered, and solutions implemented.

   - o Create diagrams, flowcharts, and reports that capture the evolution of the system.

2. **Prepare a Presentation:**

   - o Develop a slide deck or demo video showcasing the system's capabilities.

   - o Highlight key innovations, performance improvements, and real-world impacts.

Testing and Deployment

Ensuring Reliability and Performance in Real-World Scenarios

Once your autonomous system is fully integrated and optimized, rigorous testing and deployment are critical to ensure it operates reliably in real-world environments. This phase involves validating the system under various conditions, identifying potential issues, and ensuring that it meets all performance and safety requirements.

Key Testing Strategies

1. **Simulation Testing:**

   - **Controlled Environment:** Use simulation tools (e.g., Gazebo, RViz2) to test your system in a controlled virtual setting.

   - **Scenario Testing:** Simulate various scenarios such as obstacle-rich environments, dynamic changes, and sensor failures.

   - **Stress Testing:** Evaluate how the system performs under extreme conditions (e.g., high sensor noise, communication delays).

2. **Field Testing:**

   - **Real-World Deployment:** Test the system in the actual environment where it will operate.

   - **Performance Metrics:** Measure speed, latency, accuracy, and energy consumption.

   - **Safety Validation:** Verify that all safety protocols, such as emergency stop mechanisms, function as intended.

3. **Iterative Debugging:**

   - **Feedback Loops:** Continuously collect data during testing to identify issues.

- o **Incremental Improvements:** Make targeted adjustments based on test results and repeat tests until performance goals are met.

4. **User Acceptance Testing (UAT):**

   - o **Stakeholder Involvement:** Involve end-users or domain experts to evaluate the system's usability and performance.

   - o **Real-World Feedback:** Gather feedback on functionality, reliability, and user experience to guide further improvements.

Deployment Considerations

- **Scalability:** Ensure that the system can handle increased loads or be easily expanded with additional modules.

- **Maintenance:** Develop a maintenance plan for regular system updates, calibration, and troubleshooting.

- **Redundancy:** Implement redundant systems and backup protocols to handle potential failures gracefully.

- **Documentation:** Provide comprehensive documentation and user guides for future reference and training.

Hands-On Project: Comprehensive Autonomous System Build

Project Overview

In this capstone hands-on project, you will build an advanced autonomous system that integrates all the concepts you have learned throughout the book. This project will challenge you to design, implement, test, and deploy a complete system capable of navigating and operating autonomously in real-world scenarios. Your final prototype should showcase robust sensor integration, advanced perception, efficient path planning, precise control, and seamless communication.

Project Objectives

- **Integration:** Combine sensor data, perception algorithms, machine learning models, path planning, and control systems into a unified platform.

- **Optimization:** Ensure that the system operates efficiently and reliably under various conditions.

- **Testing and Deployment:** Validate the system in both simulated and real-world environments.

- **Documentation:** Produce thorough documentation outlining the design, implementation, testing, and deployment processes.

Step-by-Step Project Guide

Step 1: Define the Project Scope and Objectives

- **Mission Statement:** Clearly articulate the primary objective of your autonomous system (e.g., "Develop a mobile robot that autonomously navigates a warehouse environment while avoiding obstacles and optimizing delivery routes.")

- **Requirements:** List the technical and performance requirements, such as sensor types, processing speed, communication protocols, and operational safety standards.

Step 2: Design the System Architecture

- **Develop a High-Level Diagram:** Create an architecture diagram (similar to Diagram 1) that outlines the key subsystems.

- **Define Interfaces:** Specify how each module (sensor integration, perception, path planning, control, and communication) will interact.

- **Risk Assessment:** Identify potential challenges and develop contingency plans.

Step 3: Implement the Components

1. **Sensor Integration:**

   - Connect and calibrate sensors.

- o Develop ROS2 nodes to capture and publish sensor data.

- o Test sensor data streams and ensure synchronization.

2. **Perception and Decision-Making:**

- o Integrate deep learning models for object detection or scene analysis.

- o Implement decision-making algorithms (e.g., rule-based or reinforcement learning) to process sensor data.

- o Validate model performance using simulation data.

3. **Path Planning and Navigation:**

- o Implement path planning algorithms (e.g., A^* or RRT) to compute optimal routes.

- o Integrate dynamic re-planning capabilities to adapt to environmental changes.

- o Test path planning in both simulation and physical environments.

4. **Control and Actuation:**

- o Develop nodes to translate navigation decisions into actuator commands.

- o Ensure real-time feedback loops to adjust movements and maintain stability.

○ Test control commands for precision and reliability.

5. **Communication:**

   ○ Set up ROS2 topics, services, and actions to enable seamless data exchange between modules.

   ○ Optimize middleware settings to reduce latency and ensure robust communication.

   ○ Implement inter-module communication and error handling.

Step 4: Integrate and Test the Complete System

- **System Integration:** Merge all individual modules into a single, cohesive system.

- **Simulation Testing:** Run extensive tests in a simulated environment using Gazebo or RViz2. Validate overall system performance and identify any integration issues.

- **Field Testing:** Deploy the system on your physical robot. Monitor its behavior in real-world scenarios and adjust as needed.

Step 5: Optimize and Refine

- **Performance Profiling:** Use profiling tools to measure the system's efficiency and identify bottlenecks.

- **Iterative Improvements:** Apply optimization techniques to enhance speed, accuracy, and reliability.

- **User Feedback:** Gather input from test operators or end-users to refine the system further.

Step 6: Document and Present Your Project

- **Comprehensive Documentation:** Create detailed documentation covering system design, implementation details, test results, and optimization strategies.

- **Presentation:** Develop a presentation or demo video to showcase your project. Highlight the challenges you overcame, innovations introduced, and the overall impact of your autonomous system.

- **Lessons Learned:** Reflect on the process and document key insights and recommendations for future projects.

Summary

In **Chapter 12: Capstone Project,** we have embarked on the culminating journey of designing and building an advanced autonomous system. Here's a recap of the key elements covered:

1. **Designing an Advanced Autonomous System:**

- o Integrated all learned concepts from sensor integration to machine learning.

- o Outlined key design objectives such as robust perception, efficient navigation, and reliable communication.

- o **Diagram 1:** Provided an overview of the system architecture, highlighting the integration of various subsystems.

2. **Step-by-Step Implementation:**

- o Detailed the entire process from conception and planning to component development, integration, testing, and optimization.

- o Emphasized iterative refinement and the importance of thorough documentation.

3. **Testing and Deployment:**

- o Discussed comprehensive testing strategies including simulation and field testing.

- o Outlined best practices for performance profiling, iterative optimization, and safe deployment.

4. **Hands-On Project: Comprehensive Autonomous System Build:**

- o Provided a detailed, actionable guide to building and deploying your own advanced autonomous system.

- Covered each phase with practical steps, ensuring you can apply these concepts in a real-world project.

This capstone project is not just the end of your journey—it's the beginning of your journey into creating groundbreaking autonomous systems. It encapsulates everything you've learned and challenges you to innovate, optimize, and deploy solutions that are robust, efficient, and ready for the future.

Final Encouragement

The capstone project is your chance to showcase the culmination of your hard work and expertise. It's a test of your creativity, technical skills, and problem-solving abilities. Embrace the challenge, iterate fearlessly, and let your passion for robotics drive you to build systems that are not only functional but truly transformative. The future of autonomous robotics is in your hands—shape it, innovate it, and let it pave the way for a smarter, more connected world.

Happy building, and may your autonomous systems set new standards of excellence in robotics!

www.ingramcontent.com/pod-product-compliance
Lightning Source LLC
Chambersburg PA
CBHW080549060326
40689CB00021B/4792